Designing Legal Frameworks for Social Enterprises

PRACTICAL GUIDANCE FOR POLICY MAKERS

OECD

BETTER POLICIES FOR BETTER LIVES

This document was produced with the financial assistance of the European Union. The views expressed herein can in no way be taken to reflect the official opinion of the European Union.

This document, as well as any data and map included herein, are without prejudice to the status of or sovereignty over any territory, to the delimitation of international frontiers and boundaries and to the name of any territory, city or area.

Please cite this publication as:
OECD (2022), *Designing Legal Frameworks for Social Enterprises: Practical Guidance for Policy Makers*, Local Economic and Employment Development (LEED), OECD Publishing, Paris, https://doi.org/10.1787/172b60b2-en.

ISBN 978-92-64-77102-4 (print)
ISBN 978-92-64-56850-1 (pdf)

Local Economic and Employment Development (LEED)
ISSN 1990-1100 (print)
ISSN 1990-1097 (online)

Foreword

This manual is produced as part of the framework of the OECD Action" Designing legal frameworks for social enterprises",[1] funded by the European Union. Capitalising on the increased awareness of the potential of social enterprises to further local economic development and social inclusion, the Action analyses and explores challenges and opportunities to support social enterprise development through specific legal frameworks. This Manual provides guidance[2] to help policy makers achieve the following goals: (1) assess the rationale and relevance for developing new or updating legal frameworks specific to social enterprises; (2) analyse critical factors when designing legal frameworks for social enterprises; and (3) explore options and tools to ensure stakeholder involvement in the elaboration of legal frameworks for social enterprises as well as their assessment and evaluation.

During the Action, ten EU Member States were investigated with the objective to capture the diversity of practice, draw lessons and inspiring examples, and inform the policy making cycle in EU countries and beyond. These countries, namely Belgium, Denmark, France, Italy, Luxembourg, the Netherlands, Poland, Slovakia, Slovenia and Spain, were selected to ensure diversity among countries based on three criteria: i) the type of legal frameworks implemented to support social enterprise development, if any, ii) the regional representation across Europe, and iii) the administrative organisation of the country (unitary versus federal).

Several methods and sources of information were used to collect data in selected countries in order to support the guidance provided in the Manual:

- Literature review and desk research covered existing international, including European, national and regional reports or evaluations, academic and grey literature, policy initiatives, draft or existing laws, material from think tanks, as well as stakeholder position papers in the field of the Action.

- Expert meetings and interviews with around 80 relevant stakeholders, including policy makers at local and national level, social enterprise federations and networks, academics and legal experts, were organised in the ten selected countries. A list of the institutions involved in the expert meetings and interviews is provided in Annex A.

- A survey was prepared and diffused among the Expert Group on Social Economy and Social Enterprises (GECES), in particular its members with an expertise on the countries targeted by the Action.

Notes

[1] https://www.oecd.org/cfe/leed/social-economy/legal-frameworks.htm.

[2] In complement to this Manual, the Better Entrepreneurship Policy Tool, developed in collaboration with the European Commission, has been designed for policy makers and other interested parties at local, regional and national level who wish to explore how public policy can support the development of social enterprises in European countries and beyond. A section of the tool is dedicated to the design of enabling legal and regulatory frameworks: https://betterentrepreneurship.eu/en/node/52.

Acknowledgements

This manual was produced by the OECD Centre for Entrepreneurship, SMEs, Regions and Cities (CFE) led by Lamia Kamal-Chaoui, Director, as part of the Programme of Work of the Local Employment and Economic Development Programme. It was produced with the financial support of the European Union.

The manual was prepared by Amal Chevreau, James Hermanson and Julie Rijpens, Policy Analysts, with guidance from Antonella Noya, Head of the Social Economy and Innovation Unit and under the supervision of Karen Maguire, Head of the Local Employment, Skills and Social Innovation Division (CFE). Nadim Ahmad, Deputy Director of the OECD Centre for Entrepreneurship, SMEs, Regions and Cities (CFE) provided comments and suggestions. Additional research and legal analysis was provided by the Thomson Reuters Foundation. The authors thank OECD colleagues Daniel Bayram, Viktoria Chernetska, Jozef Cossey, Sweekrity Goyal and Marine Hasson for their inputs and help in collecting background information.

Authors further thank all respondents to the survey and participants to the expert meetings, interviews and webinars for their inputs in the discussion. The document benefitted from valuable comments provided from Céline Kauffmann, Head of Entrepreneurship SME and Tourism Division (CFE), Marie Boscher, European Commission (DG GROW), Julien De Beys, European Commission (DG EMPL) as well as the Advisory Board, namely Giulia Galera (Euricse), David Hiez (University of Luxembourg), Peter Holbrook (Social Enterprise UK), Roberto Randazzo (Legance - Avvocati Associati) and Suzanne Wisse-Huiskes (European Social Enterprise Network).

Authors are also grateful to Erica Weathers for designing the infographics and cover design, and to Pilar Philip and Kristin Sazama for preparing the manual for publication.

This document was approved and declassified for publication by the Local Employment and Economic Development Programme Directing Committee on 5 April 2022.

Table of contents

Tables

Figures

Boxes

Executive summary

There is strong potential for social enterprises to promote and advance inclusive and sustainable growth and offer opportunities to many groups to create economic activities with social impacts. Social enterprises have grown in prominence and expanded their reach across the globe. However, their potential is still not fully exploited. Awareness and evidence need to be built around how legal frameworks, tailored or not, can effectively unlock this potential.

The number of social enterprises has increased in recent decades. In the European Union, based on national-level data, there are roughly 397 000 social enterprises with variation among member states (European Commission, 2020[1]). For example, Belgium, Hungary, Italy and Luxembourg have over 1500 social enterprises per million inhabitants, whereas Estonia, Greece and Malta have less than 500 (European Commission, 2020[1]). Due to multiple definitions and varying degrees of legal recognition for social enterprises, the quality of data on social enterprises differs between countries and even subnational regions.

There is growing legal recognition of social enterprises. In the EU, 16 countries having adopted some form of legislation specific to social enterprises over the past two decades. Countries have pursued a variety of approaches tailored to their specific domestic conditions and needs of social enterprises. While some countries have adopted legislation creating specific legal forms for social enterprises (e.g. Italy, the United Kingdom), others have created legal statuses available to one or several legal forms that meet specific criteria (e.g. Denmark, Luxembourg, Slovenia). Likewise, countries have also utilised fiscal frameworks for social enterprises, with some awarding tax exemptions to specific legal forms or creating fiscal incentives for individuals to donate or invest in social enterprises.

Despite improved legal frameworks for social enterprises, many entities continue to operate as *de facto* social enterprises. For example, in some jurisdictions, foundations or associations may be allowed to partake in market-based activities; cooperatives to benefit the general interest by addressing the needs of non-members; and limited liability companies (LLCs) to pursue a social purpose and implement constraints on profit-distribution to the shareholders. In this case, these entities, while effectively operating as social enterprises, may lack legal recognition as such, which may prevent them from accessing support programmes and inhibit the overall growth of the social enterprise ecosystem. It also makes it challenging to accurately estimate their number in a given country, region or city.

OECD research indicates that with adequate design and effective implementation, legal frameworks can be a powerful tool to foster and bolster social enterprise development. Legal frameworks may support social enterprises develop and thrive by clarifying what they are and what authorities can do to best tailor legal provisions to meet their needs (Haarich et al., 2020[2]). Italy and Poland, for example, saw significant increase in the number of social cooperatives after the introduction of specific legal frameworks. OECD work also shows that countries can choose not to adopt legal frameworks. In this case, they need to leverage other mechanisms to support social enterprise development such as tax policy, action plans and strategies.

The Manual for Legal Frameworks for Social Enterprises provides policy makers with policy guidance to design and implement effective legal frameworks to promote social enterprise development. Developing and adopting legal frameworks can be a complex and time-intensive process. This Manual helps policy makers identify the right time to develop legal frameworks and provides comprehensive steps to successfully adopt and implement them. It equips policy makers with concrete guidance to make the most of legal frameworks, by highlighting notable practices mainly collected from ten EU countries, which leverage legal frameworks to support social enterprises in most cases.

Taking into account different EU Member State contexts, the Manual focuses on:

1. Legal options governing social enterprises when legal frameworks explicitly recognise them;
2. Essential features of a social enterprise – in line with the OECD and European Commission definitions – and the criteria to qualify as a social enterprise;
3. Factors that support policy making processes to design legal frameworks as well as the features to be considered when assessing the performance of these legal frameworks.

The Manual is complemented inspiring practices and experiences from EU and OECD countries to unveil challenges, gaps and opportunities regarding regulations for social enterprises. Finally, it identifies potential criteria to assess legal frameworks performance. It takes into consideration the criteria used in the European Commission / OECD "Better Entrepreneurship Policy Tool" and complementary work such as OECD Framework for Regulatory Policy Evaluation, which assists countries in evaluating the design and implementation of regulatory policy, against the achievement of strategic regulatory objectives.

References

European Commission (2020), *Social enterprises and their ecosystems in Europe. Comparative synthesis report*, Publications Office of the European Union, https://ec.europa.eu/social/main.jsp?catId=738&langId=en&pubId=8274. [1]

Haarich, S. et al. (2020), *Impact of the European Commission's Social Business Initiative (SBI) and its Follow-up Actions*, European Commission, Luxembourg. [2]

1 Why a Manual on Designing legal frameworks for social enterprises?

There is growing legal recognition of social enterprises across the globe. Over the past two decades, 16 EU countries (e.g. France, Denmark, Italy, Luxembourg, and Spain) have adopted some form of legislation on social enterprises to identify them as such. Although the other 11 EU countries have not done so they have designed explicit policies or strategies to boost their expansion (European Commission, 2020[1]).

Social enterprises are active in a broad range of sectors, offering innovative solutions to pressing challenges. For example social enterprises help to address: demographic changes linked to ageing populations (e.g. Italy, Luxembourg); climate change; regional development, and revitalisation of remote communities (e.g. Slovakia, Spain); care activities, education, community development, environment and energy, social housing (e.g. France), migrant integration (e.g. France, Spain). They are also active in work integration activities, (WISEs, work integration social enterprises) (European Commission, 2020[1]). The ongoing recovery from the COVID-19 pandemic provides an opportunity to leverage on the potential of the social economy, including in collaboration with public and private partners, to further local economic development and support more sustainable and inclusive economies and societies (OECD, 2020[2]).

Legal frameworks have a significant impact on the visibility, recognition, identity and organisation of social enterprises and act as important enablers of their development. The primary and most common justification for designing legal frameworks specific to social enterprises is the inadequacy of most existing legal frameworks to grasp the specific features of business models that they use which in turn, can act as a barrier to their development. Business models used by social enterprises can be generally characterised by i) the priority pursuit of community or general interest, ii) a continuous economic activity and an entrepreneurial dimension, iii) asset locks that ensure assets, including profits generated by the activities, are partly retained within the organisation and not fully distributed to capital owners, and iv) inclusive governance models.

However, existing legislation on other legal entities captured in the broader notion of the social economy are not always well equipped to reflect these models. For example, legislation regulating cooperatives can prohibit them from addressing the needs of non-members, i.e. pursuing a general interest. Legislation on associations often prevents them from engaging in market activities. Legislation regulating limited liability companies may prevent them from explicitly pursuing a social purpose and limiting the distribution of profits. Likewise, existing legal statuses in some countries suitable for certain categories of social enterprises, e.g. WISEs, may be too restrictive regarding the social needs that these organisations are meant to pursue.

In practice, social enterprises use various legal forms and legal statuses that reflect their diverse entrepreneurial approaches. Some of these legal forms and statuses have been designed specifically to recognise social enterprises and support their development (e.g. France, Luxembourg or Slovenia). Social enterprises can also take legal forms and statuses which have not been designed specifically for them, such as WISEs' legal statuses or legal forms such as associations or cooperatives.

Legislation which specifically recognises and regulates social enterprises (Box 1.1) gives them a clear, distinct and protected legal identity, which might have positive impacts (Fici, 2017[3]; Fici, 2015[4]; OECD/EUCLID, 2020[5]) namely: i) clearer boundaries with other entities or more general concepts (e.g. SME's and traditional entities or enterprises of the social economy; corporate social responsibility); ii) legal identification and recognition that could facilitate the collection of more reliable official statistics and data ; iii) the improvement of the conditions in which they operate through targeted public support schemes and specific public policies, such as tax incentives, public procurement and financial and non-financial assistance and benefits.

Box 1.1. What is referred to by "Legal frameworks" in this Manual?

In the context of this Manual, the term "legal framework" or "legal framework specific to social enterprises" is used to refer to legislation adopted specifically to recognise social enterprises through suitable legal forms or legal statuses. These legal texts may include provisions to:

- define the specific features of the legal form or legal status created by the legal framework, as well as the list of criteria an entity must follow to be recognised under this legal framework,
- clarify the possible financial and fiscal benefits attached to this new legal form or status,
- organise the evaluation of the legal framework on a regular basis, possibly indicating the actors to be involved,
- in some cases, define the social (and solidarity) economy or the third sector as a broader phenomenon in which social enterprise is recognised as one dynamic.

Legal frameworks specific to social enterprises introduce legal forms or legal statuses:

- A legal form is the foundational legal structure adopted by an organisation, e.g. association, cooperative or limited liability company (European Social Enterprise Law Association, 2015[6]). Legislations that define legal forms establish specific purposes and set specific rules on the ownership, governance structure as well as distribution of profit (e.g. social cooperatives in Italy and in Poland);
- A legal status can be adopted by a number of legal forms based on the compliance with certain criteria such as the primacy of social purpose, a stable and continuous production of goods and services or limited profit distribution (OECD, 1999[7]). A legal status has an impact on the treatment, e.g. fiscal, of those legal forms (European Social Enterprise Law Association, 2015[6]). Several countries have adopted such legal statuses, like Denmark, Luxembourg and Slovenia.

References

European Commission (2020), *Social enterprises and their ecosystems in Europe. Comparative synthesis report*, Publications Office of the European Union, https://ec.europa.eu/social/main.jsp?catId=738&langId=en&pubId=8274. [1]

European Social Enterprise Law Association (2015), *Social Enterprise in Europe. Developing Legal Systems which Support Social Enterprise Growth*, ESELA.   [6]

Fici, A. (2017), *A European Statute for Social and Solidarity-Based Enterprise*, European Union.   [3]

Fici, A. (2015), "Recognition and Legal Forms of Social Enterprise in Europe: A Critical Analysis from a Comparative Law Perspective", *Euricse Working Papers*, Vol. 82/15.   [4]

OECD (2020), *Social economy and the COVID-19 crisis: current and future roles*, OECD Publishing.   [2]

OECD (1999), *Social enterprises*, OECD Publishing.   [7]

OECD/EUCLID (2020), *Webinar: OECD Global Action to Promote the Social and Solidarity Economy*.   [5]

2 Guidance on legal frameworks for social enterprises

This section provides practical step-by-step guidance on the critical stages for designing regulation for social enterprises. Guidance is organised around three phases related to the life cycle of legal frameworks: 1) a scoping phase; 2) a development phase and 3) an evaluation/assessment phase.

- The **scoping phase** outlines legal definitions of social enterprises and helps policy makers to identify when to regulate social enterprises and understand why it can be beneficial to do so under certain conditions.

- The **development phase** outlines how to navigate the often challenging policy making process while developing legal frameworks to meet stakeholder needs and remaining attuned to institutional constraints and achieve consensus. It presents different options and approaches to social enterprise regulation and fiscal policy measures countries leverage to develop the field.

- The **evaluation phase** presents possible actions policy makers can take to anticipate the important, but often overlooked, evaluation process to ensure the long-term success of legal frameworks for social enterprises. It also explores avenues to adopt a dynamic perspective of legal frameworks to further develop social enterprises.

Each of these phases is broken down into distinct and, at the same time, intertwined steps that policy makers are likely to encounter when designing legal frameworks for social enterprises. By providing straightforward guidance to address these steps along with best-practice examples and useful tools, this section helps policy makers navigate the challenges that they are likely to encounter throughout the process of designing legislative frameworks for social enterprises.

Figure 2.1. Designing legal frameworks for the social enterprises: a process in three phases

Scoping Phase
Why and when to regulate social enterprises
1 Why support social enterprise development?
2 What is a social enterprise and how to legally define it?
3 Why and when to regulate social enterprises?

Development Phase
Crafting a policy-making process and leveraging legal and fiscal tools
4 Securing a successful policy-making process
5 Achieving consensus and co-ordinating policy
6 Ensuring stakeholder inclusion
7 Regulating social enterprises: trends and options
8 Leveraging fiscal policy for social enterprises

Evaluation Phase
Assessing the performance of legal frameworks and adapting them to evolving needs
9 Assessing legal framework performance
10 Adopting a dynamic perspective of legal frameworks

Source: Authors' elaboration

Scoping phase: Why and when to regulate social enterprises

Step 1 - Why support social enterprise development?

Social enterprises are an important and expanding component of the social economy. Social enterprises and social economy organisations are important drivers for job creation and account for roughly 6.3% of all jobs in the European Union (CIRIEC, 2017[1]). They account for annual economic turnover of EUR 2.3 billion in Hungary, EUR 37.3 billion in Italy, EUR 3.5 billion in the Netherlands and EUR 3.3 billion in Portugal (European Commission, 2020[2]). Like other social economy organisations, social enterprises utilise innovative approaches to achieve certain social objectives more effectively than purely public or private sector actors thanks to their pioneering business models and local orientation and knowledge (OECD, 2013[3]).

These specificities enable social enterprises to promote job creation, social and economic inclusion, local economic development and the green transition (OECD, 2020[4]; OECD/European Commission, 2022[5]; OECD, 2018[6]). For example, in the United Kingdom, social enterprises employed roughly 5% of the national workforce in 2017 and contributed GBP 60 billion to the economy as a whole (Social Enterprise UK, 2018[7]). Moreover, many social enterprises such as work integration social enterprises (WISEs) prioritise hiring vulnerable or marginalised groups who would otherwise struggle to find employment. As a consequence, supporting the development of social enterprises can enable policy makers to tackle social challenges more efficiently that would otherwise be possible. For example, Spain promoted social enterprises as a way to offset the effects of the 2008 global financial crisis, fiscal austerity and high unemployment.

The COVID-19 pandemic highlighted the adaptability of social enterprises. The COVID-19 pandemic led to social distancing measures such as curfews, school closures and teleworking. These necessary public health measures disrupted global supply chains and challenged the business models of social enterprises and traditional businesses alike. To adapt to these challenges, social enterprises around the world rapidly adapted their business operations by digitising their operations and developing new services or products such as medical equipment (Borzaga and Tallarini, 2021[8]; British Council, 2020[9]). In the United Kingdom, 44% of social enterprises reported increased turnover since the onset of the COVID-19 crisis compared to 18% of traditional businesses, and only 35% reported decreased in turnover compared to 56% of traditional businesses during the same period (Social Enterprise UK, 2021[10]). A global survey conducted by the British Council (2020[9]) estimates that only 1% of social enterprises were forced to permanently close to the COVID-19 crisis. This capacity to quickly adapt to rapidly changing operating conditions and spiralling demand for assistance enabled social enterprises around the world to weather the crisis while contributing to the welfare of their communities (OECD, 2020[11]). It is no coincidence that several European countries, such as Belgium, France, Ireland, Luxembourg and Spain, recognise this potential in their recovery and reform packages.

Social enterprises possess the resilience to survive economic crises while continuing to contribute to the welfare of their communities. In certain countries, employment in social enterprises grew during the 2008 global financial crisis, with employment in social enterprises growing by 20.1% in Belgium and 11.5% in Italy between 2008 and 2010 (OECD, 2018[6]). More recently, social enterprises showed similar resilience in the face of the COVID-19 pandemic, with only 1% of social enterprises surveyed across 38 countries forced to close due to disruptions caused by the crisis (British Council, 2020[9]). As such, social enterprises contribute to overall social and economic resilience in the face of unexpected economic shocks.

Box 2.1. Australia: Driving social enterprise development at the subnational level through alternative policy frameworks

Australia is a federal country with a mixed landscape of social enterprises incorporated under a variety of legal forms that are regulated by different levels of government. At the federal level, there is no legal framework specifically designed for social enterprises and states lack the competency to adopt state-level legal frameworks. Given the varying extent of support measures provided by state governments, the growth of the social enterprise field across Australia is uneven. However, state governments, the federal government and other stakeholders are creating considerable momentum towards the development of a comprehensive policy framework for social enterprises at the state and federal level.

Even in the absence of specific legal frameworks for social enterprises, subnational governments have demonstrated their potential in supporting their development. States have been supporting social enterprises through a variety of measures that reflect their specific needs and policy objectives. The states of Victoria and Queensland are two pioneering and proactive states that

---

have taken measures to promote social enterprise development through strategies, policy measures and funding.

Victoria launched Australia's first Social Enterprise Strategy in 2017. The strategy led to numerous capacity and network building initiatives, such as the government-supported creation of the Social Enterprise Network Victoria (SENVIC) that connects social enterprises across Victoria, provides access to learning and development opportunities, and facilitates engagement with government and intermediaries. Additionally, the launch of the whole-of-government Victorian Social Procurement Framework in 2018 facilitated access to markets for social enterprises, including through adjusting the size of contracts as well enhancing the knowledge and skills of both buyers and suppliers. Building on the strong foundation of the first Social Enterprise Strategy, later iterations of the Strategy (currently running from 2021 to 2025) helped to grow the social enterprise field, enabling it to play a greater role in creating jobs and delivering social and economic value.

The policy agenda set by the Victorian government inspired the subsequent development of strategies for social enterprises in various states such as in Tasmania, Queensland and New South Wales. In 2019, Queensland's government launched a social enterprise strategy to support the development and growth of social enterprises through targeted support in the areas of capacity building, network creation and access to markets. Following this, in 2021 the government of Queensland announced plans to allocate AUD 8 million to the Social Enterprise Jobs Fund, which supports, amongst other initiatives, the roll-out of several grant programmes for the benefit of social enterprises and intermediary organisations.

Source: (Barraket et al., 2017[12]; Barraket, Mason and Blain, 2016[13]), 2019 Queensland Social Enterprise Strategy, 2017 Victoria Social Enterprise Strategy, 2021-2025 Victoria Social Enterprise Strategy, (Queensland Government Department of Employment, n.d.[14])

Step 2 - What is a social enterprise and how to legally define it?

Social enterprises benefit economies and societies by supporting local economic development and job creation while driving social inclusion (see Step 1 - Why support social enterprise development?). Public authorities that recognise these social and economic benefits may develop some form of targeted support for social enterprises, which requires authorities to define which entities can be considered as social enterprises in order to qualify for support schemes. Therefore, defining the social enterprise is a necessary step when designing specific legal frameworks.

What is a social enterprise?

A **social enterprise** is any private entity whose activity is conducted in the general interest, organised with an entrepreneurial strategy, whose main purpose is not the maximisation of profit for the sake of personal enrichment but its use for the attainment of certain economic and social goals. It has the capacity for bringing innovative solutions to social problems, among which social exclusion and unemployment (OECD, 1999[15]). According to this perspective, social enterprises emerge within the social economy[1] and extend its scope beyond its traditional legal forms, namely the associations, the cooperatives, the mutual organisations and the foundations. Like any social economy organisation, social enterprises distinguish themselves in two respects: their *raison d'être*, as they primarily address societal needs and maximise their social impact, and their *way of operating* because they implement specific business models based on collaboration, typically at the local level (OECD/European Commission, 2022[5]). Box 2.2 presents the European concept of the social enterprise and its operationalisation for the recent European mapping study on the social enterprise ecosystems (European Commission, 2020[2]).

Box 2.2. The European concept of the social enterprise

According to the Social Business Initiative, a social enterprise is an operator in the social economy whose main objective is to have a social impact rather than make a profit for their owners or shareholders, and that operates by providing goods and services for the market in an entrepreneurial and innovative fashion and uses its profits primarily to achieve social objectives. It is managed in an open and responsible manner and, in particular, involves employees, consumers and stakeholders affected by its commercial activities (European Commission, 2011[16]). The social purpose of a social enterprise may also include environmental goals (European Union, 2021[17]).

Relying on the EMES International Research Network approach to social enterprises (Borzaga and Defourny, 2001[18]) and building on the OECD definition, the European Commission established that social enterprises "run commercial activities (entrepreneurial/economic dimension) in order to achieve a social or societal common good (social dimension) and have an organisation or ownership system that reflects their mission (inclusive governance-ownership dimension)" (European Commission, 2011[16]) As presented in the table below, these dimensions have been further operationalised in the framework of the European Commission mapping study on the social enterprise ecosystems in Europe (see note below).

Main dimension	General definition	Minimum requirements
Entrepreneurial/economic dimension	Stable and continuous production of goods and services. • Revenues are generated mainly from both the direct sale of goods and services to private users or members and public contracts. (At least partial) use of production factors functioning in the monetary economy (paid labour, capital, assets). • Although relying on both volunteers (especially in the start-up phase) and non-commercial resources, to become sustainable, social enterprises normally also use production factors that typically function in the monetary economy.	Social enterprises must be market-oriented (incidence of trading should be ideally above 25%).
Social dimension	The aim pursued is explicitly social. The product supplied/activities run have a social/general interest connotation. • The types of services offered or activities run can vary significantly from place to place, depending on unmet needs arising at the local level or in some cases even in a global context.	Primacy of social aim must be clearly established by national legislations, the statutes of social enterprises or other relevant documents.
Inclusive governance-ownership dimension	Inclusive and participatory governance model • All concerned stakeholders are involved, regardless of the legal form. • The profit distribution constraint (especially on assets) guarantees that the enterprise's social purpose is safeguarded.	The governance and/or organisational structure of social enterprises must ensure that the interests of all concerned stakeholders are duly represented in decision-making processes.

Note: https://ec.europa.eu/social/main.jsp?catId=738&langId=en&pubId=8274
Source: (European Commission, 2020[2])

While sharing common principles and practices, social enterprises, like the wider social economy, show a great diversity in terms of legal entities, size, outreach and sectors. Social enterprises are recognised through a diversity of legal forms and statuses to capture entrepreneurial approaches within the social economy. **A majority of social enterprises are small and medium-sized entities active in a wide range of sectors throughout the economy** (Figure 2.2), but the field also includes examples of large entities and groups of social economy organisations whose size reaches that of multinationals in some cases, such as the Mondragon cooperative group in Spain and the *Groupe SOS* in France.

Figure 2.2. Social enterprises are active in various sectors

Social enterprises, and the social economy at large, are active in a wide range of sectors throughout the economy.

Source: Adapted from (OECD, 2020[11]).

How are social enterprises legally defined?

The term "social enterprise" is rarely used *per se* in legal frameworks but a range of countries recognised, under specific designations, new forms of entrepreneurship that correspond to the notion of social enterprises. *De jure* social enterprises are those legally recognised under specific legal frameworks that create suitable legal forms and statuses designed specifically to support the social enterprise development (such as the *solidarity enterprise of social utility (ESUS)* in France, the *societal impact company* in Luxembourg, or the *social cooperative* in Poland). **De facto social enterprises** are not legally recognised through legal forms and statuses specific to social enterprises but can be considered as such because they produce important services of general interest and operate along the same specific features than social enterprise business models.

Social enterprises can take a diverse set of legal forms and statuses that reflect their specific dimensions, namely their entrepreneurial/economic approaches, their social objectives, and their inclusive governance - or ownership status. In a strict legal sense, social enterprises are more of an operational model (Caire and Tadjudje, 2019[19]). Countries have adopted a number of approaches to recognise social enterprises, operationalise these specific features and ensure these entities operate as such. Box 2.3 gathers inspiring examples of definitions used in legal frameworks.

- *Social dimension*:
    - Legal frameworks stipulate that social enterprises must explicitly pursue a designated social objective. Certain countries define the fields of engagement in which social enterprises are

expected to operate. In Luxembourg, Societal Impact Companies must be active in one of the sectors enumerated in Art. 1 of the 2016 Law on Societal Impact Companies (European Commission, 2020[20]). Likewise, the 1991 Italian Law on Social Cooperatives requires the entities to be active in A-list activities (health care, environmental protection, and enhancement of cultural heritage) or B-list activities (organisations that conduct entrepreneurial activity oriented to job inclusion of disadvantaged or disabled workers/people, regardless of the sector or area).

– In many countries, social enterprises are requested to respect a partial or full asset lock in order to preserve the social purpose on the long run and prioritise social impact in decision-making processes. The asset lock may include two mechanisms: a constraint of non-distribution or limited distribution of profits to the owners, and a constraint to transfer any surplus on liquidation to a similar initiative in case of dissolution. For example, Belgium, France, Italy, Luxembourg and the United Kingdom have introduced such limitations on the amount of profits that can be redistributed to the owners or shareholders.

- *Entrepreneurial and/or economic dimension*: Legal frameworks may explicitly indicate that social enterprises pursue a continuous activity of production, distribution or exchange of goods or services (e.g. to distinguish them from some other types of social economy actors), while specifying some criteria to capture this dimension, such as a certain amount of revenues from sales or a certain level of paid work.

- *Inclusive governance and/or ownership*: Some legal frameworks on social enterprises require the participation of workers in the decision-making process. For example, French companies with an ESS-label or ESUS legal status (recognised by the French Law on the Social and Solidarity Economy of 2014) are required to organise participation of stakeholders in some company decisions.

Box 2.3. Inspiring examples – Defining social enterprises in legal frameworks

Belgium, Brussels-Capital Region

Based on the EMES International Research Network approach of the social enterprise (Borzaga and Defourny, 2001[18]), the 2018 Brussels Ordinance [1] defines the 'social enterprises' as private or public legal entities that implement an economic project, pursue a social purpose, and exercise democratic governance. These three dimensions are further operationalised through a set of criteria that apply differently to public and private legal entities. Private legal entities, for example, can be recognised as a social enterprise if they respond positively and cumulatively to the following principles:

- (Art. 4) the implementation of an economic project is characterised by:
    - a continuous activity producing goods and/or selling services;
    - an economically viable activity;
    - a minimum amount of paid work which is of quality and lasting;
- (Art. 5) the pursuit of a social purpose is characterised by:
    - the inscription in the act of incorporation of an explicit objective to develop activities and/or services that aim to benefit the community or a specific group of individuals;
    - the priority given to the social purpose by limiting profit distribution and by implementing sustainable production and consumption methods;
    - the demonstration of a moderate wage tension [2];
- (Art. 6) the exercise of a democratic governance implies:

- – a high degree of autonomy in strategic orientations as well as in daily management;
- – a democratic decision-making power not based on the sole capital ownership;
- – a transparent and participatory dynamic involving the main stakeholders.

France

The 2014 Law on the Social and Solidarity Economy [3] and the Labour Code define the cumulative conditions that an entity must follow to be recognised with the "solidarity enterprise of social utility" legal status (*entreprise solidaire d'utilité sociale* – ESUS), which include that:

- the enterprise primarily pursues a social utility [4], as defined in the Law on the Social and Solidarity Economy;
- the charge entailed by the social utility purpose has a significant impact on the profit and loss account or on the financial profitability of the enterprise;
- the remuneration policy implies a moderate wage tension (which is explicitly defined in the Law);
- the capital shares, when existing, may not be negotiated on the French or a foreign financial market;
- Conditions 1) and 3) are explicitly mentioned in the act of incorporation.

Luxembourg

According to the 2016 Law on Societal Impact Companies [5], any public limited company, limited liability company or cooperative that meets the social and solidarity economy's principles defined in Article 1 of the Law can be recognised as a societal impact company. The social and solidarity economy is a form of entrepreneurship to which private legal entities adhere if they fulfil the following conditions:

- Pursue a continuous activity of production, distribution or exchange of goods or services.
- Meet primarily at least one of the following two main conditions:
  - They aim to provide, through their activity, support for people in vulnerable situations, either because of their economic or social situation, or because of their personal situation and particularly their state of health or their need for social or medico-social support. These persons may be employees, customers, members, subscribers or beneficiaries of the company;
  - They aim to contribute to the preservation and development of social ties, the fight against exclusion and health, social, cultural and economic inequalities, gender equality, the maintenance and reinforcement of territorial cohesion, environmental protection, the development of cultural or creative activities and the development of initial or continuing training activities.
- To be autonomous in the sense that they are fully capable of choosing and dismissing their governing bodies and of controlling and organising all their activities.
- Apply the principle that at least half of the profits generated are reinvested in the maintenance and development of the company's activity.

The act of incorporation must also meet some requirements, namely (1) to define precisely the social purpose; and (2) to provide the performance indicators that will enable the effective and reliable assessment of the social purpose's achievement. Additional criteria include, among others, the obligation to maintain a moderate wage tension (from 1 to 6 times the minimum social wage), the requirement to establish an extra-financial impact report and the need to transfer any liquidation surplus to another societal impact company pursuing a similar social purpose or to a Luxembourg-based foundation or public benefit association.

Poland

The 2006 Law on Social Cooperatives [6] stipulates that the objective of social cooperatives is to run a joint venture based on the personal work of its members and employees. The Law requires that social cooperatives:

- Operate to achieve the social and professional reintegration of its members and employees;
- May carry out social, educational and cultural activities for their members, employees and their local environment, as well as socially useful activities in the sphere of public tasks as defined in the Act of 24 April 2003 on public benefit activity and on voluntary work (Journal of Laws of 2020, item 1057);
- Can be founded by natural persons or at least two legal person (e.g. local governments, charities or non-profit organisations);
- May not distribute profits among their members or use profits to increase the social cooperatives equity fund. Profit gained should be divided between the fund dedicating the cooperative's activities (*fundusz zasobowy*), reintegration activities for members and employees of the social cooperative, and a mutual fund (*fundusz wzajemnościowy*).

Note:
[1] http://www.ejustice.just.fgov.be/eli/ordonnance/2018/07/23/2018031816/justel
[2] In an organisation, the wage tension is the gap between the lowest wages and the highest ones.
[3] https://www.legifrance.gouv.fr/loda/id/JORFTEXT000029313296/
[4] Entities are recognised as pursuing a social utility if their social purpose fulfils primarily at least one of the three following conditions: (1) to support vulnerable groups through their activities; (2) to contribute to fight against sanitary, social , economic and cultural exclusion and inequalities, to citizenship education, to preservation and development of social and territorial cohesion; (3) to contribute to sustainable development in its economic, social, environmental and participatory dimensions, to energy transition or to international solidarity (2014 Law on Social and Solidarity Economy, Art. 2).
[5] https://legilux.public.lu/eli/etat/leg/loi/2016/12/12/n1/jo
[6] http://isap.sejm.gov.pl/isap.nsf/download.xsp/WDU20060940651/U/D20060651Lj.pdf

Sources: 2014 Law on the Social and Solidarity Economy (France), 2016 Law on Societal Impact Companies (Luxembourg), 2018 Ordinance on Social Enterprises (Brussels-Capital Region, Belgium), 2006 Law on Social Cooperatives (Poland), (European Commission, 2020[21])

Guiding questions for policy makers

Policy makers need to answer four questions to develop a legal definition of the social enterprise that aligns with their objectives:

- **Why define the social enterprise?** Defining the social enterprise is a necessary step when designing legal frameworks in order to identify clearly which entities can be considered as such. Societal and economic benefits of social enterprises are increasingly recognised alongside the need to support their development through specific measures. This requires the ability to clearly identify social enterprises in order to clarify which entity can benefit from these measures but also to ensure that support is effectively targeted in a way that enables existing social enterprises to fully leverage on that status and encourages other firms to adopt it.
- **What to define?** *De facto* social enterprises might already exist in the field, i.e. entities that adopt the specific features of the social enterprises and operate as such. The legal definition of the social enterprise may adopt an encompassing approach that recognises both these pre-existing *de facto* social enterprises and newly-established social enterprises. This approach is recommended to ensure clarity within the field and consistency among diverse support schemes.
- **How to define?** Defining social enterprises in a strategy with the purpose of shedding light on this field will not require the same level of detail as defining social enterprises in a legal framework to

clarify precisely which entity may benefit or not from targeted support measures. Different approaches can be used to define social enterprises. The most common approach consists of defining principles and operationalising these principles to clearly establish which entity may be recognised as a social enterprise, and which may not. Another option consists of setting criteria to define the social enterprises' specific features or fields of engagement in which social enterprises are expected to operate, albeit at the risk of restraining social enterprises to certain sectors of activity.

- **With whom to define?** Various actors in the field may have developed a practice (e.g. *de facto* social enterprises) or a corpus of knowledge (e.g. researchers, international organisations) on social enterprises. To represent the field's sensibilities, it is preferable to include social enterprises' founders and managers, in addition to social enterprise networks and federations, to better capture the realities and needs on the ground. Paying attention to include actors that represent the diversity of the social enterprise field is also critical. Policy makers should consider involving these actors in the discussion when defining the social enterprise, which can enrich the perspective and ensure alignment with social enterprises' realities in the country.

Step 3 - Why and when to regulate social enterprises?

Legal frameworks can act as strong enablers for social enterprise development, but countries could also choose not to adopt them. Legal frameworks are an important ecosystem policy tool. They legitimise social enterprises and enlarge the legal concept of "enterprise" to entities that twin an entrepreneurial approach with social and increasingly environmentally motivated missions. The trend to adopt legal frameworks stems from the growing interest of many EU national and subnational authorities in social enterprises alongside other forms of social economy entities due to their primary focus on public and/or general interest and capacity to support the implementation of specific policies (social and green) and strategic priorities such as job creation for disadvantaged groups. However, some EU countries choose not to adopt them. Instead, they use working definitions and/or criteria embedded in strategies, action plans, to identify social enterprises and design specific policy tools including tax policy to support their development.

Four actions should guide the decision to regulate:

- **Assessment** of the need for legal frameworks based on local contexts, especially when substantive rules are coupled with policy measures of a fiscal nature (Fici, 2017[22]);
- **Identification** of the benefits of regulation for the development of social enterprises;
- **Anticipation** of the potential implications of regulation;
- **Evaluation** of the right moment to regulate social enterprises.

Figure 2.3. Actions to guide the decision to design legal frameworks for social enterprises

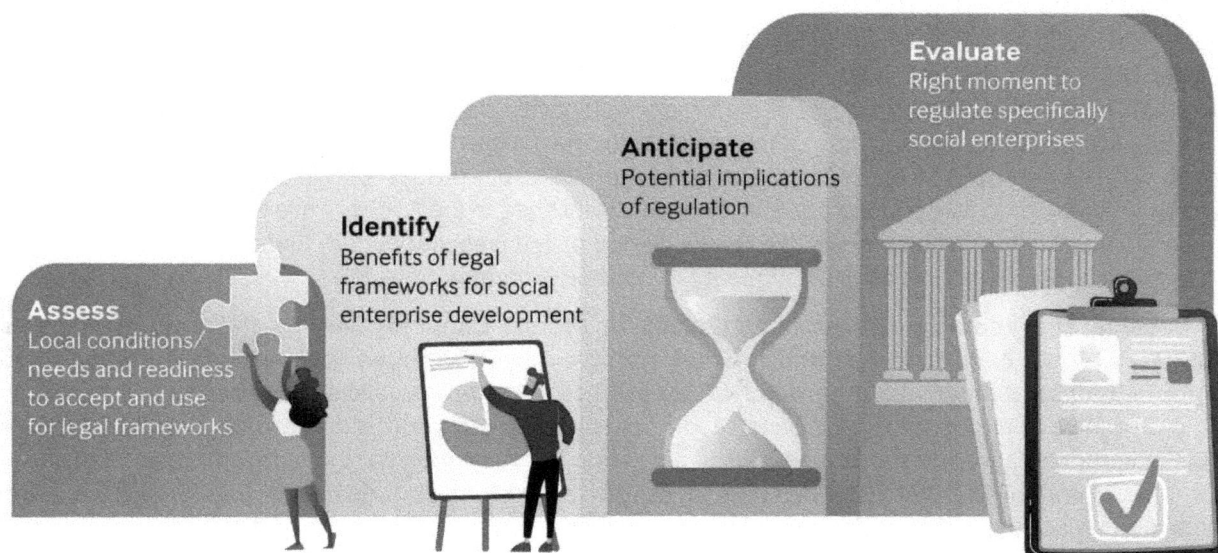

Source: Authors' elaboration

1- Assessment of the need for legal frameworks

The need for legal frameworks for social enterprises is often assessed based on national/local needs and contexts. A range of factors motivate the need to design legislation for social enterprises. Such factors include: i) the expansion of enterprises that pursue a social mission and economic objectives (e.g. France); ii) the dynamism of social enterprise networks that actively advocate for recognition through legal frameworks (e.g. Italy, the Netherlands); iii) demands for recognition of social enterprises from local governments to facilitate collaboration and transfer of service provision (e.g. Denmark); iv) the need to design specific fiscal and public support policies and programmes tailored to social enterprises (e.g. the Brussels Capital Region in Belgium) and vi) the need to clearly identify the distinctive features of social enterprises to attract patient capital and funders that could guarantee their sustainability (OECD, 2009[23]).

For example, in France, the 2014 Law on the Social and Solidarity Economy recognises social enterprises (Box 2.4). This legal recognition was spurred by the rise, in the early 2000s, of a new generation of entrepreneurs wishing to prove that economic efficiency can be combined with social objectives such as social justice (*entreprendre autrement*); a thriving social economy and ecosystem and social enterprise, mainly from the work integration field and more globally the engagement of social economy organisations such as associations and production cooperatives in the production of general interest services to the benefit of non-members. The "solidarity enterprise of social utility" or "socially useful solidarity-based enterprise" status (*entreprise solidaire d'utilité sociale – ESUS*) was introduced and open to all legal forms. It gives access to specific support and financial schemes, such as solidarity employee savings (solidarity finance) and tax breaks. (European Commission, 2020[24]).

In Denmark, the expansion of strategies for social enterprises at municipal and local level contributed to the adoption of the Act on Registered Social Enterprises in 2014 (Box 2.4). The adoption of such strategies contributed to their acknowledgment as important partners of local authorities and led to the adoption of the Act on Registered Social Enterprises in 2014. The 2014 Act established a voluntary registration system for social enterprises to help them get greater access to potential customers, investors and partners. Being registered meant being more visible, thus facilitating potential fiscal incentives or specific support to social enterprises. The Registration tool also helped to support changes to public welfare systems while facilitating the necessary efficiency and innovation to address complex and increasingly diversified needs arising in society (European Commission, 2019[25]).

In Italy, the first Law on Social Cooperatives adopted in 1991 is the outcome of networks' advocacy for legal recognition (Box 2.4). The need for legislation was expressed by stakeholders themselves. In addition, within some regions (e.g. Trentino Alto Adige), regional laws on social cooperatives were introduced before Law 381 on Social Cooperatives in 1991, but always with initiatives from cooperative networks. The first social cooperatives in Italy were established in the 1960s, while the law was introduced almost 20 years later. When the Law on Social Cooperatives was introduced, there were already around 500 social cooperatives operating throughout the country (Borzaga, Scalvini).[2]

In Slovakia, the adoption of the Act 112/2018 on Social Economy and Social Enterprises was instigated by the need to define and register social enterprises to facilitate access to finance and improve their credibility with the public. Under this Act, social enterprises are embedded in the broader context of the social economy with clear conditions to be fulfilled in order to be recognised as *"de jure* social enterprises". Organisations fulfilling a set of conditions may apply for the status of "registered social enterprise" through which they can benefit from a wide range of support measures. Based on the act, the social enterprise is not a specific legal entity, but rather a status that may be obtained by various legal entities, including both non-profit organisations, and conventional enterprises. Most social economy actors can register as social enterprises (European Commission, 2020[26]).

In Spain, the 2008 economic crisis, public fiscal austerity, as well as high unemployment and cuts in welfare state provision were the main drivers for the recognition of the concept of social enterprise as part of the social economy in the Law 5/2011 on the Social Economy. Supporting structures, such as social entrepreneur programmes and private initiatives for encouraging social initiatives have acted as catalysts for the emergence for new forms of social enterprises, where entrepreneurs engage in economic activities with clear social aims and within a participatory decision-making process (European Commission, 2020[27]).

Box 2.4. Examples of countries with specific legislation on social enterprises

France

The Law on the Social and Solidarity Economy, adopted in 2014, explicitly defines the conditions that an entity must meet to qualify as a "social enterprise of social utility". By establishing this specific label, the law creates favourable conditions for social enterprise development. In the 2000s, social economy organisations, mainly WISEs, started to speak about social entrepreneurs and/or social enterprises to capture the evolution of organisations that try to achieve more sustainable economic models with a social mission. Over the same period, the debate on social enterprise was enriched by the discussion on the introduction of a new cooperative form that allows for expanding the cooperative purpose beyond the sole mutual interest: the *société coopérative d'intérêt collectif* (SCIC). Introduced in 2001, this cooperative legal form also helped to spur the expansion of social cooperatives in France.

Denmark

Denmark is a highly regulated welfare state where the extensive public supply of social services is increasingly contracted out. This increased the recognition of social enterprises and boosted their development. The origin of "social enterprise" in Denmark can be traced back both to the mid- to late-1800s farmers' and workers' cooperative movements and to the emergence of voluntary associations and non-profit organisations a few decades later. Both the "socialist workers' movement" and the "*Grundtvigian movement*" have been highly influential in the thinking of both old and new types of social enterprises. The late 1960s was a particularly influential period in the cultivation of the modern social enterprise, both through the expansion of a new era of social work reforms and evolution of an institutional and universally oriented welfare state and through the emergence of social initiatives more related to new social movements than to the cooperative movements and the traditional third-sector. This helped spark a new wave of social economy composed by local, bottom-up activities.

The concept of social enterprise started only to gain public attention and influence after 2000. This increased attention culminated around 2013-2014 when the Act no. 711/2014 on Registered Social Enterprises was introduced to create the Registered Social Enterprise (RSV) status. Applicants must meet specific criteria regarding their social objectives, profit distribution, and governance model, among other criteria.

Italy

Social cooperatives were recognised as social enterprises long after their development. When the reflection on social enterprises started, the need of social cooperatives and other third sector actors was to use economic tools to tackle new social needs, which needed more developed capital aggregation and productive organisation models that the social cooperatives model could not provide at that time. Social cooperatives are characterised by slow capital aggregation. In addition, the democratic governance model of social cooperatives would not allow to develop partnerships. Therefore, actors in the social economy were looking for a refined legal instrument which would allow co-operation among equals, but also involving "diverse" organisations, including through the involvement of local stakeholders, public institutions and private institutions (but still preserving a concept of autonomy). Additionally, Legislative Decree 112/2017 made the legal status of "social enterprise" available to commercial companies as well as to not-for-profit organisations such as associations and foundations.

Sources: (European Commission, 2020[24]; European Commission, 2019[25]; European Commission, 2020[28]), Focus group discussion "France" (16 October 2020), Focus group discussion "Italy" (18 December 2020); Focus group discussion "Denmark" (4 February 2021), https://www.legifrance.gouv.fr/jorf/article_jo/JORFARTI000029313713.

In other countries, regulating social enterprises has not been the priority. The non-readiness of the ecosystem to accept or comply with legislation (see Box 2.5); opposition and/or resistance to regulation and potential negative effects of legal frameworks might motivate the decision of not designing legal frameworks for social enterprises. **In the absence of legal frameworks, authorities need to specify the criteria that identify a social enterprise in a policy document or an administrative decree**.

For example, in the Netherlands**, there is currently no dedicated legal framework for social enterprises**. The absence of specific legislation for social enterprises stems from the longstanding involvement of the private sector in public service delivery and the structural decentralisation reforms (European Commission, 2019[29]). Existing accountability mechanisms are deemed adequate to monitor firms' commitment to social missions and distribution of profits, partly due to the Netherlands' stakeholder model. The Dutch model recognises that corporations depend on stakeholders for success and have a corresponding responsibility to them. This follows a 1949 ruling by the Dutch Supreme Court which stated that company boards should not only act in the shareholders' interests. In 1971, the Dutch civil code was amended to reflect that boards must act in the interests of the company and its business. This amendment confirmed that boards should not only look at the interests of shareholders, but also of other stakeholders, including particularly employees. These interests materialise through three actions: (i) embedding a clear stakeholder mission in the fiduciary duties of the board, (ii) giving teeth to that stakeholder mission, while creating appropriate checks and balances, and (iii) fostering a stakeholder-oriented mind-set and environment (Christiaan de Brauw, Allen & Overy, 2020[30]).

There is also reluctance to create tax exemptions or other benefits for social enterprises that could undermine the level playing field between social enterprises and traditional firms. Despite the absence of national legislation, municipalities developed action plans and leveraged public procurement to support social enterprises, when responsibility for some welfare provisions were shifted from the national to the municipal level (OECD, 2019[31]). For example, Amsterdam adopted a three-year Action Plan for Social Entrepreneurship in late 2015 (Oetelmans, 2015[32]). This Action Plan provided a clear definition of social enterprises and outlined 17 measures to help understand and measure the social enterprise ecosystem and improve support systems through a variety of specific steps ranging from conducting surveys and obtaining quantitative data to study the benefits of allocating municipal funds to support social enterprises (Amsterdam Impact, 2017[33]).

In Poland, entities identified as social enterprises[3] are regulated by specific legal frameworks for each legal form. There is no commonly agreed legal definition for social enterprises, but it has been introduced in practice. **The National Programme for Social Economy Development (KPRES) 2019-2023, introduced a set of criteria to help recognise social enterprises**. They are identified as entities which conduct market activities, including both economic activity and paid mission-related activity aimed at the reintegration socially excluded groups; which must be at least 30% of the workforce. Moreover, social enterprise status entails democratic governance, profit distribution constraints and salary caps (European Commission, 2020[34]). KPRES also helped to streamline policy making processes related to social enterprises by delineating responsibilities between the national and regional level, helping to facilitate stronger co-ordination. In this respect, policy makers can act to support social enterprises in a co-ordinated manner despite the absence of a single specific legal framework for social enterprises as a whole.

Box 2.5. Ireland: Exploring the possibility to adopt a dedicated legal form for social enterprises

In July 2019, the Irish Government's Department of Rural and Community Development introduced the National Social Enterprise Policy 2019-2022, which includes a definition of social enterprises but also acknowledges that further research on legal forms for social enterprises is needed. To this end, Rethink Ireland and the Department of Rural and Community Development commissioned a research study that consulted policy makers, social enterprises, network organisations and academics in order to gain insights on the barriers experienced by social enterprises as they relate to legal form, as well as the benefits and necessity of creating a dedicated legal form for social enterprises. Ultimately, the study did not recognise the need for a distinct legal form for the following reasons:

Many of the barriers identified were less to do with legal form, and more to do with compliance, access to resources, governance, visibility and recognition of social enterprises. The majority of the Irish social enterprises surveyed agreed that a dedicated legal form would resolve many issues and provide a fit-for-purpose form that could facilitate the future development of the field. However, the majority (59%) of respondents also believed that their current legal form meets their current and future needs. There was also a view that some of the identified barriers could be alleviated by greater use of existing legal forms, such as those of a company, an association, a cooperative, or hybrid structures reflecting both for-profit and not-for-profit components of a social enterprise. Moreover, respondents held very different views regarding the features that a dedicated form would comprise.

Additionally, issues relating to clarity about social enterprises and simplifying governance systems would remain to be addressed, irrespective of whether or not a specific legal form was adopted. Finally, the task of establishing a relatively permanent legal form would imply a significant and lengthy undertaking. Considering all this, the study recommended utilising other policy levers to support social enterprises before seeking to adopt a dedicated legal form based on the development of the field.

Sources: (Government of Ireland, 2019[35]; Lalor and Doyle, 2021[36]; Thomson Reuters Foundation and Mason Hayes & Curran LLP, 2020[37])

---

2. Identification of benefits of legal frameworks for social enterprise development

Legal frameworks can have benefits for social enterprise development. The adoption of legal frameworks usually signals that social enterprises are important to authorities. In most countries (e.g. France, Italy, Luxembourg), where legal frameworks for social enterprises were introduced, they brought four major benefits:

- *Clarity by defining the nature, mission and activities of such enterprises.* An enshrined definition approved by the Parliament carries more authority than a working definition.[4] It identifies and recognises the specific features of social enterprises which facilitate their recognition and visibility. A legal definition cannot be easily revised in the event of political change, as this require a formal process to amend it. In addition, a legal definition may also spur a movement of entrepreneurs seeking to start a business with social impact.

- *Design of policy levers to promote social enterprises*. The existence of legal frameworks leads to differentiated legal regimes and support for the entities identified. Such support may take different forms: tax and fiscal arrangements; tailored access to public procurement; access to suitable and targeted public funding schemes; reduction of incorporation and registration costs; specific incentives to encourage employment of specific groups (e.g. disadvantaged or disabled people). In addition, entities that are legally recognised as social enterprises know what is legally required from them to qualify for public support.

- *Better understanding of what social enterprises are and how they operate vis-à-vis funders and authorities.* The clear labelling provided by a law helps identify the potential benefits of investing in and/or collaborating with social enterprises. This can also encourage investors to support their social mission. Social enterprises are built for and prioritise their social/societal mission over profit-maximisation and this is secured in their legal form or statutes through various mechanisms (e.g. profit caps, non-distributable profit reserves, etc.).

- *Identification of social enterprises in the entrepreneurial continuum.* Social enterprises are entities oriented towards generating social impact. As such, they should be distinguished from traditional businesses which are primarily accountable to their owners or shareholders in terms of profit redistribution. Social enterprises should also be distinguished from non-profits or citizens' initiatives that do not provide goods and services for the market in an entrepreneurial manner. They also differ from traditional cooperatives because of their aim - promote the interests of non-members - and constraint on profit distribution.

Figure 2.4. Advantages and disadvantages of legislation for social enterprises

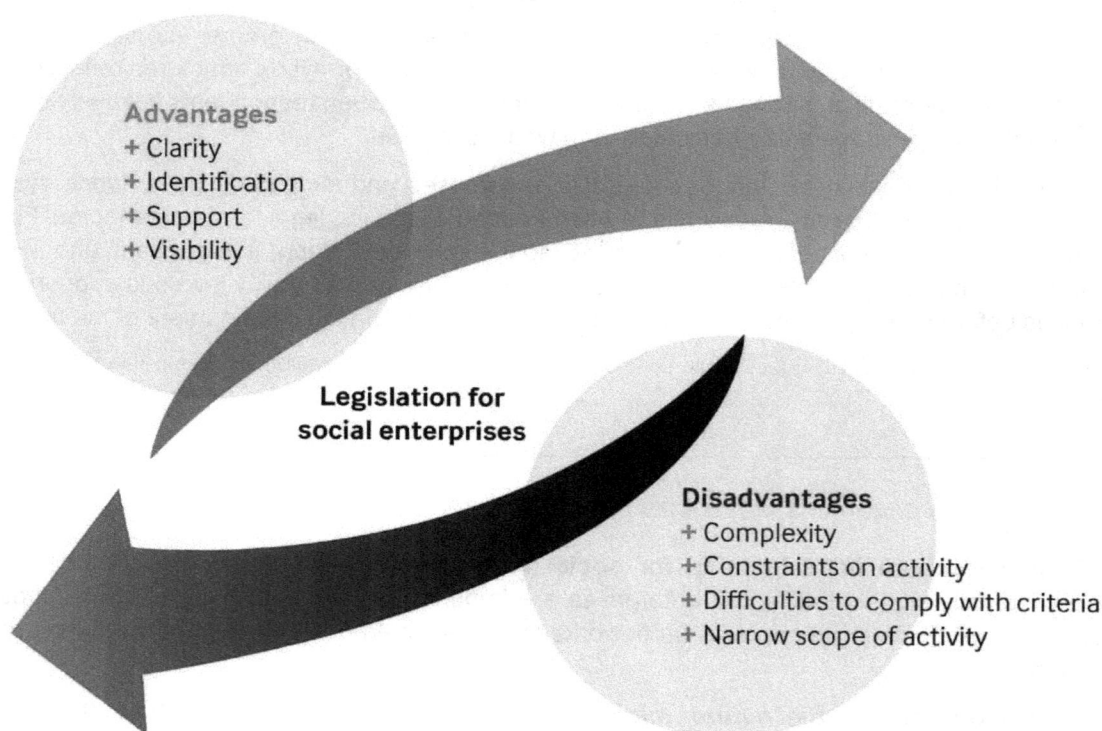

Advantages
+ Clarity
+ Identification
+ Support
+ Visibility

Legislation for
social enterprises

Disadvantages
+ Complexity
+ Constraints on activity
+ Difficulties to comply with criteria
+ Narrow scope of activity

Source: Authors' elaboration

Box 2.6. Colombia: *De facto* social enterprises in the absence of legal frameworks

In Colombia, it is common to find cooperatives operating as *de facto* social enterprises, i.e. organisations that are not legally constituted as social enterprises but that share the principles and mission of social enterprises in practice. These *de facto* social enterprises can be found in sectors such as in the financial, savings, and credit sector; agriculture, livestock, and food industries; commercialisation and consumption; insurance, transport; and social services and health, among others. The latest performance report published by Confecoop, the confederation of cooperatives in Colombia, underlines the relevance and impact of this type of organisations and indicates that cooperative services reach all 32 departments of Colombia through 3 205 active cooperatives accounting for nearly 6.3 million members and 139 093 direct jobs in the country (Confecoop 2018 records).

Although Colombia does not have a legal framework on social enterprises, it does have a rich body of cooperative legislation. Since 1988, Colombia has adopted laws and regulatory decrees aiming at the formalisation, growth, monitoring, and control of the cooperative sector. The law 79 of 1988 and the law 454 of 1998 were fundamental for cooperatives and solidarity economy in Colombia, as they established conceptual frameworks and rules for the regulation of these organisations and the overall solidarity economy. These laws (and those following them) created different supervisory bodies, and although cooperatives are mainly monitored and supervised by the Superintendency of the Solidarity Economy (i.e. highest institutional authority that administers and regulates this type of organisations), the supervision of cooperatives may fall under other superintendencies depending on the economic activity in which the cooperative is engaged.

The legislative framework led to the creation of different promotion and control bodies with differentiated objectives and interests, which made cross-government co-ordination to support the growth of cooperatives and the solidarity economy challenging. Legal frameworks sometimes pose challenges for social economy organisations, and the Colombian Government is aware of this. Colombia is currently taking steps towards improving their legal frameworks, as they recognise the great potential of social and solidarity economy organisations to tackle important challenges for the country, such as reducing labour and business informality, among many others.

Source: (Hernández Salazar and Olaya Pardo, 2018[38]; International Labour Office (ILO), 2019[39])

---

3 – Determining when to specifically regulate social enterprises

Identifying the 'right' time to create new legal frameworks for social enterprises is also context dependent. It should be supported and informed by the development of the social enterprise ecosystem in a given country, region or city.

As adopting legal frameworks is often a complex and time-intensive process, it may be preferable to pursue other policy levers before proposing new legal frameworks. Designating specific government institutions to support social enterprise development or developing fiscal measures, financial support instruments, and public procurement regulations that benefit social enterprises are effective ways to spur social enterprise development that typically do not require the same investment of time and political capital as legal frameworks. Alternative fiscal policy options are discussed in greater detail in Step 8.

It is often advisable to wait until the social enterprise ecosystem is well-developed, hosting social enterprises with a diverse array of business models, legal forms and social objectives. The level of development and overall dynamism of the social enterprise ecosystem matter. Introducing legal frameworks that regulate social enterprises before the ecosystem has time to develop may create unnecessary barriers that may constrain social enterprise development by, for example, discouraging them from operating in certain sectors or adopting specific legal forms. Consequently, while legal frameworks introduced early on may benefit a subset of social enterprises, they may be detrimental to the development of the overall social enterprise ecosystem.

If the social enterprise ecosystem is well-developed and there is demand to specifically regulate social enterprises, it is generally a signal that it may be time to develop a legal framework. As previously discussed, legal frameworks that provide social enterprises with legal recognition or specific legal forms can help to facilitate visibility, legitimacy, access to finance and access to markets for social enterprises, among other benefits. Working with a diverse set of stakeholders and policy makers across government can help to identify how to achieve these potential benefits while avoiding the possible downsides of new regulations that could inhibit the development of the social enterprise ecosystem.

If the political will to develop legal frameworks for social enterprises is missing, awareness raising efforts may be necessary before seeking to develop legal frameworks. Widespread public support must be met by political support among government institutions and elected officials. In some target countries, critical ministries were initially resistant to creating specific legal forms for social enterprises for fear of undermining fair competitive conditions *vis-à-vis* social enterprises and traditional businesses. Only after successfully awareness raising efforts by social economy associations and other advocates for legal frameworks did the attitudes shift, opening the possibility to regulate social enterprises.

On the other hand, some countries have successfully developed legal frameworks early on during the development of their social enterprise ecosystems. Slovakia adopted a legal framework for social enterprises through the adoption of the Act on Social Economy and Social Enterprises (Act 112/2018) even though the social enterprise ecosystem was still in a relatively early stage of development. Despite this timing, creating a specific legal status for social enterprises stimulated their development by enabling greater access to markets and access to finance, namely to European Structural Funds, and helping to rehabilitate public perceptions of social enterprises following a corruption scandal in 2008. However, although the number of social enterprises increased by over 650% between 2019 and 2022 following the introduction of the Act, almost all registered social enterprises operated as WISEs. While the Act successfully encouraged social enterprise development, it has not yet helped to promote the development of new types of social enterprises as it was introduced early on during the development of the social enterprise ecosystem. This example highlights the importance that countries pursue policy options suited to their specific needs as well as the potential trade-offs between different policy options.

4 – Anticipation of the implications of regulation for social enterprises

When designing legal frameworks for social enterprises, it is important to consider and accommodate the positive and also potential secondary effects of legislation on social enterprise development but also on the social economy more globally and on traditional enterprises.

Positive implications

- **Regulating** may raise awareness of the field and give social enterprises greater legitimacy and access to finance and markets (e.g. Slovakia).
- **Not regulating** may enable the field to develop organically without constraints imposed by public authorities (e.g. the Netherlands).

Potential secondary effects

- **Legal frameworks can impede social enterprise development if unclear or excessively narrow.** Legal frameworks which introduce many criteria and/or an unclear or complex definition might enhance confusion around social enterprises or fail to clearly identify entities that may qualify as such in a given context. Regulations may also affect the competitive balance between social enterprises and traditional firms.

- **The lack of a legal definition** could lead to different and potentially inconsistent definitions or criteria by the various institutions involved in providing support to social enterprises.
- **This is why policy makers should consider solutions based on local contexts**: adapting or adjusting existing legislation on specific legal forms – for instance cooperatives – or designing new laws. Less rigid normative tools could be considered if easier to implement.

Lessons learnt

- **Policy makers need to develop clear understanding of why, when and how to regulate** social enterprises and the impact that legislation (or lack thereof) can have for their development.
- **The need for regulation for social enterprises is context-based**: motives and outcomes of legal frameworks reflect local conditions, which means that what works within the broader legal and regulatory frameworks of one country may not in another and vice versa.
- **Legal frameworks may provide recognition, visibility,** as well as access to financial incentives and support, to markets, and to support services which facilitate starting, developing and growing social enterprises.
- **Without a law, authorities need to separately define** the criteria that make up a social enterprise, in a relevant policy document or administrative decree.
- **The costs and benefits of legal frameworks need to be assessed and accommodated** when designing legislation for social enterprise but also on the social economy more globally and on traditional enterprises.
- **Just as legal frameworks can help unleash the potential of social enterprises, they can also be a source of constraints** that restrict social enterprises to specific activities or types of business models. It is imperative that stakeholder views are considered throughout the development process in order to develop forward-looking legal frameworks that meet stakeholder needs.
- **Top-down regulations and policies** risk constraining social enterprise development to specific sectors or business models.
- **The timing of proposed legal frameworks matters**. Policy makers should consider the maturity and development of the social enterprise ecosystem, among other variables, as they can affect the viability of legislative proposals.

Figure 2.5. Important steps for the scoping phase

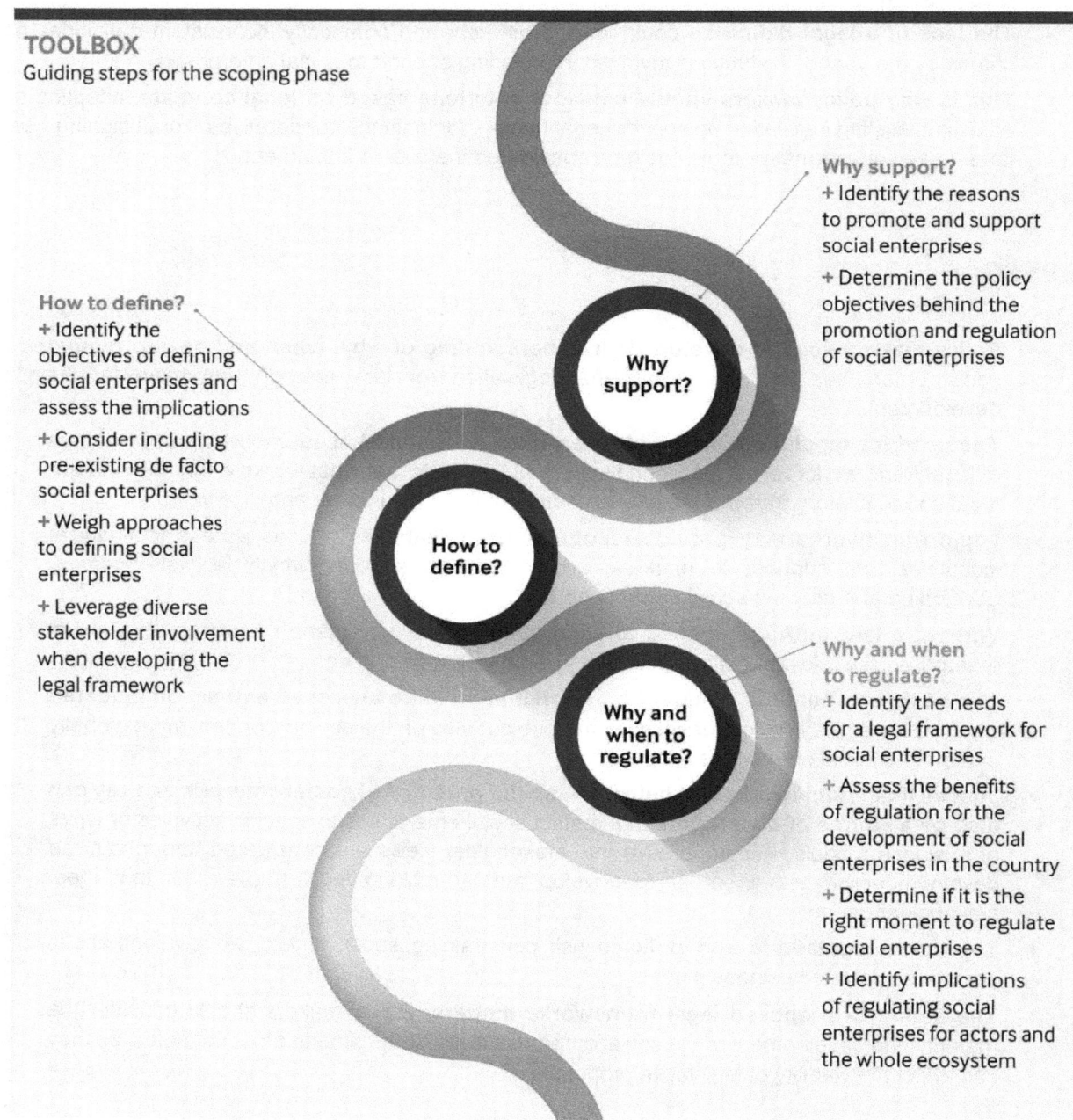

TOOLBOX
Guiding steps for the scoping phase

Why support?
+ Identify the reasons to promote and support social enterprises
+ Determine the policy objectives behind the promotion and regulation of social enterprises

Why support?

How to define?
+ Identify the objectives of defining social enterprises and assess the implications
+ Consider including pre-existing de facto social enterprises
+ Weigh approaches to defining social enterprises
+ Leverage diverse stakeholder involvement when developing the legal framework

How to define?

Why and when to regulate?
+ Identify the needs for a legal framework for social enterprises
+ Assess the benefits of regulation for the development of social enterprises in the country
+ Determine if it is the right moment to regulate social enterprises
+ Identify implications of regulating social enterprises for actors and the whole ecosystem

Why and when to regulate?

Source: Authors' elaboration

Development phase: Crafting a policy-making process and leveraging legal and fiscal tools

Step 4 - Securing a successful policy-making process

Policy makers face an often complex and time-intensive process to develop and adopt new legislation for social enterprises. Unlike other policies, altering existing legal frameworks or developing new ones involves a lengthy legislative approval process that may span multiple legislative chambers and voting procedures. Given this complexity, it is important to understand the successive phases of developing legal frameworks and proactively develop a plan to navigate them and secure the desired legislative outcome.

Legislative frameworks have to meet the needs of stakeholders and align with the preferences of critical institutions and legislators. Striking a balance between the preferences of these three groups – stakeholders, government institutions and elected officials – requires identifying and engaging with important partners and the national, regional and local level early on is an important way to assess support for new legislation. It is vital to engage with stakeholders (such as social entrepreneurs and social enterprise associations, among others), government institutions, and elected officials early in the process. Doing so provides a basis with which to assess support for new laws or regulations among elected officials, government ministries and stakeholders and adapt the design and advocacy processes accordingly.

Many successful efforts to regulate social enterprises have hinged on support from crucial ministries or networks. Identifying influential supporters of new legislation can help to build coalitions (discussed in greater detail in Step 7) and facilitate the adoption process. However, over-relying on support from specific ministries (and indeed, often individuals) can ingrain certain biases into the legal framework. In some countries, legislation that received strong support from the Ministry of Employment was disproportionately focused on promoting work-integration social enterprises. Consequently, although a legal framework that promoted social enterprises was successfully adopted, its focus on WISEs ultimately deterred the establishment of other types of social enterprises focusing on addressing social issues beyond employment and the inclusion of vulnerable individuals in the labour market.

Adopting a structured approach early in the legislative process helps build momentum by identifying sources of support and opposition and avert disruptions by adapting the proposed legislation to stakeholder needs and institutional constraints. This ensures that legal frameworks are politically viable while adequately accommodating stakeholder needs. However, it is also important to adopt a forward-looking approach that encourages monitoring and evaluation of the new legislative framework to ensure that it fully meets the needs of social enterprises once it is adopted.

Lessons learnt

- **Adopting legal frameworks often involves a complex and time-intensive process:**
  - **It is important to consider the timing of new legislative proposals** in relation to the maturity of the social enterprise ecosystem and the potential costs and benefits of 'early' action.
  - **Successful legal frameworks typically align with the vision of stakeholders, government institutions and elected officials.** It is important to communicate with stakeholders from each of these groups to understand their respective positions and needs.
  - **Support from crucial ministries or networks can be integral in successfully adopting legal frameworks.** Though not always necessary, finding partners to champion legislative proposals can help build momentum and attract support, but care is needed to avoid biases promoting narrow policy priorities at the expense of the overall social enterprise ecosystem.

Step 5 - Achieving consensus and co-ordinating policy

Placing social enterprises on the political agenda is a critical step towards achieving the necessary consensus to adopt legal frameworks. Winning political support for new social enterprise legislation and regulations can be challenging. This is further complicated by often narrow understandings of what social enterprises are, how they operate, and the kind of benefits they offer. In certain target countries, social enterprises were traditionally understood to primarily benefit labour markets by offering work integration and training opportunities to vulnerable individuals who would otherwise struggle to obtain employment. As noted in the previous section, achieving consensus limited to these areas can produce legal frameworks that ultimately constrain the development of social enterprises. It is thus important to help policy makers understand the diverse specificities, benefits and needs of social enterprises in order to generate a consensus beyond areas such as the social or employment sectors.

It is also important to ensure horizontal (across departments) and vertical (across levels of government) co-ordination. Achieving consensus across government institutions to adopt comprehensive legal frameworks for social enterprises creates its own set of co-ordination challenges.

- **Horizontal co-ordination:** If multiple government ministries and other institutions are responsible for implementing specific aspects of the legal framework, a lack of horizontal co-ordination could lead to inconsistent or even contradictory approaches. Designating a ministry or government institution to oversee social enterprise policy or establishing a formal mechanism to co-ordinate policy across multiple ministries can help to avoid such issues. In Luxembourg, the Law on Societal Impact Companies (2016) established strong horizontal co-ordination mechanisms that facilitated cross-ministry communication and collaboration. These proved important to harmonising policy implementation and, later, identifying and revising conflicting legal frameworks. Annex E provides detailed information on the legal framework for social enterprises in Luxembourg.

- **Vertical co-ordination:** Different levels of government may adopt different approaches and even legal frameworks for social enterprises. Subnational governments in both federal and centralised states have acted to support social enterprises through direct support as well as by developing subnational regional frameworks. In France and the Netherlands, among other countries, cities such as Amsterdam, Lille, and Grenoble developed grants and public procurement processes to support social enterprises. In some OECD countries, such as Canada, the federal system of government enabled provinces to establish their own legal forms for social enterprises such as Community Contribution Companies in British Columbia and Community Interest Companies in Nova Scotia. These examples highlight the variety of ways in which local and regional governments can act autonomously to support social enterprises. At the same time, this risks creating a jurisdictional patchwork of distinct operational environments within the same country that may enhance confusion and inhibit the development of social enterprises at the national level. As such, it is important to engage with all levels of government to facilitate communication and develop legal frameworks that minimise potential vertical co-ordination issues that may hinder social enterprise development while still empowering subnational governments to help social enterprises meet their distinct needs.

Building consensus and establishing policy co-ordination help to ensure policy maker engagement in the design, implementation and evaluation stages of the policy-making process. While both steps are time and resource intensive processes, they promote stronger commitment to implementing policies related to social enterprises as well as the social economy at large. In France, a number of mechanisms helped build consensus and achieve policy co-ordination while driving engagement in the development and implementation stages of the legal framework for social enterprises. The creation of the Interministerial Delegation for Innovation, Social Experimentation and the Social Economy in 1981 (*Délégation interministérielle à l'innovation, à l'expérimentation sociale et à l'économie* sociale) provided a forum where policy makers across the French government could discuss the social economy. During the development of the 2014 Law on the Social and Solidarity Economy (*Loi sur l'économie sociale et solidaire*), this interministerial committee played a formative role in building consensus and facilitating horizontal communication on the social economy and its individual components, including social enterprises. French regions also utilise regional social and solidarity economy councils that formulate policies for the social economy at the regional level. This practice helps to ensure vertical co-ordination between subnational and national government institutions and policy makers.

It is important to ensure the coherence of legal frameworks for social enterprises with other laws as they may contradict existing legislation. Building consensus among relevant parties and facilitating communication among them is a useful way to proactively identify potential legislative conflicts while the legal framework is under development. However, in many cases, such legislative conflicts are not identified until after legal frameworks are adopted. One way to address potential legal conflicts is to identify them through dedicated studies and to engage with the relevant stakeholders to collect their perspectives on how they can be addressed.

Establishing policy maker commitment ensures that such conflicts are identified and resolved as the legal framework is implemented once it has been adopted. In countries such as Luxembourg a formal process to identify and resolve contradictions with existing legislation or policies across the government was adopted. Please refer to Annex E for more information on this mechanism.

Lessons learnt

- **Gaining political support and building consensus among elected officials and governments for legal frameworks is a challenging but necessary step,** which often requires raising awareness about the specific social and economic benefits of social enterprises as well as their specific needs.
- **Horizontal and vertical co-ordination are important for the successful design and implementation of legal frameworks.** This helps to proactively identify potential conflicts with existing legal frameworks and harmonise policy across government.
- **Sustained engagement by policy makers across government is vital for the long-term success and adaptability of legal frameworks.** This helps to address eventual conflicts with other laws or policies and facilitates changes to the legal framework to meet evolving stakeholder needs over time.

Step 6 - Ensuring stakeholder inclusion

While developing legal frameworks through a top-down policy-making process may be easier to organise, it risks ignoring the needs of stakeholders. In some target countries that did not prioritise stakeholder inclusion, policy makers adopted laws and regulations that did not meet the full range of needs of social enterprises. Top-down policy-making processes risk not only ignoring the needs of stakeholders, but also engraining narrow understandings of social enterprise into law. As a consequence, while these legal frameworks may have helped certain social enterprises, they constrained the development of the overall social enterprise ecosystem to specific legal forms, sectors, or types of activity. It can take time and substantial resources to adapt legal frameworks once they have been adopted, which means that the consequences of an initial failure to collect stakeholder inputs can continue to shape social enterprise development for years or even decades.

Collecting inputs from a diverse array of stakeholders helps to ensure that legal frameworks are responsive to their real world needs. Target countries have utilised a range of methods to bring relevant stakeholders to the table and collect their views on proposed legal frameworks. For example, the

Netherlands allowed stakeholders to provide feedback on a draft legislative proposal to create a legal status for social enterprises. By publishing the proposed legislation and providing an opportunity for stakeholders to share feedback, this approach to stakeholder involvement enables interested parties to identify potential issues or limitations with the legal framework before it is adopted into law. One potential downside of this approach, however, is that it does not engage stakeholders from the beginning of the development phase of the law and only passively collects inputs rather than actively incorporating a deliberately diverse array of stakeholders. As discussed in Box 2.3, the inclusive policy-making process utilised by the Brussels-Capital Region in Belgium to develop its 2018 Ordinance on social enterprises enabled stakeholders to provide inputs through a two-year consultation process.

Box 2.7. Case study – The Brussels 2018 Ordinance on social enterprises (Belgium): an inclusive policy-making process to co-construct a legal framework for social enterprises

The Ordinance on the accreditation and support of social enterprises was adopted on 23 July 2018 in the Brussels-Capital Region in Belgium. The adoption of this Ordinance resulted from a two-year consultation process with various stakeholders, including the Economic and Social Council of the Brussels-Capital Region (CESRBC), the Brussels Employment Office Actiris, the Brussels Social Economy Consultation Platform extended to ConcertES and SAW-B. Additional stakeholders, such as academics, social enterprise federations and individual social enterprises, also participated in the consultation process.

Until 2018, social enterprises and other social economy organisations active in the Brussels-Capital Region were largely associated with the work integration field. Hence, the objective of the policy-making process was twofold: (1) the revision of the 2004 and 2012 Ordinances on the social economy and the accreditation of work integration social enterprises; and (2) the recognition of social enterprises beyond the work integration field.

Throughout all stages of the two-year long development of the ordinance, relevant stakeholders were involved through consultations, direct participation in expert discussions and surveys. As a result, the 2018 Ordinance establishes a set of criteria organised in three dimensions – social, economic and governance – and defines 'social enterprise' as private or public legal entities that implement an economic project, pursue a social purpose, and exercise democratic governance.

By starting the consultation process at an early stage of policy development, the Government of the Brussels-Capital Region was able to collect valuable information from a variety of stakeholders to better capture the situation experienced by work integration social enterprises but also to refine their understating of the needs and realities of social enterprises working on issues beyond work integration. Such an inclusive process fostered the dialogue between policy makers and main actors in the field, and allows to easily gather these main actors around a table when needed. In short, the Brussels Ordinance on social enterprises and its policy-making process helped to both build common understanding of social enterprises and structure the overall field, which in turn fostered the development of social enterprises in the Brussels-Capital Region.

The complete case study available in Annex B further describes the policy-making process, its benefits to include diverse stakeholders as well as the challenges.

It is important to understand and accommodate the full range of stakeholders during the legal framework development process. As noted in Step 2, social enterprises utilise a range of legal forms that include associations, cooperatives, charities, foundations, and mutual societies. These might also include conventional enterprises, such as limited liability companies, specific types of non-profit organisations (e.g. *Zavodi* in Slovenia) and public benefit companies (e.g. the Czech Republic) (European

Commission, 2020[2]). Identifying and incorporating these diverse legal forms, business models and social objectives into the stakeholder consultation process helps to ensure that legal frameworks meet the ever evolving, real-world needs of social enterprises. Countries that have limited their stakeholder consultations to well-established types of social enterprises such as WISEs while excluding emerging or less prevalent types of social enterprises ultimately developed legal frameworks that met the specific needs of a subset of social enterprises. This ultimately constrained the development of the overall social enterprise ecosystem by not encouraging the development of novel legal forms, business models and social objectives.

If legal frameworks for social enterprises are already in place, it is important to accommodate the views of social enterprises not yet explicitly recognised by law. Social enterprises can operate as *de jure* and *de facto* social enterprises depending on whether they are legally recognised as a social enterprises within a given country or region. Consequently, it is important to engage with both *de jure* and *de facto* social enterprises in order to identify whether existing legal frameworks unnecessarily exclude *de facto* social enterprises from legal recognition and constrain the development of the overall social enterprise ecosystem.

Social enterprise networks, lobbying groups and other representative bodies can help to identify relevant stakeholders and facilitate outreach. These social enterprise networks (e.g. MOUVES in France or Social Enterprise Netherlands in the Netherlands) are an important resource that can enable policy makers to access the views of a diverse range of social enterprises from a single source. As such, it can be beneficial to engage with them early on in the development process to collect feedback and identify which types of stakeholders are present. It is important to note that the composition of social enterprises associations and other representative bodies varies, and they may represent only a subset of social enterprises within a given country or region.

Box 2.8. Who to reach out to and how? A checklist for stakeholder inclusion

This box identifies the range of social enterprises that may exist in a given country to help policy makers engage with a diverse range of stakeholders when develop new legal frameworks for social enterprises. Likewise, this box provides an overview of the various ways in which policy makers can engage with stakeholders during the development process.

Critical stakeholders

- Social enterprises from a diverse range of:
    - Common legal forms
    - Business Models
    - Social Objectives
- Social enterprise networks
- Academia
- National and subnational policy makers

Tools for Inclusion

- **Surveys disseminated among social enterprises and social enterprise associations:** Surveys are a useful way to gather preliminary information on the needs and challenges faced by social enterprises. One advantage of surveys is that they can be quickly shared across social enterprise networks or targeted at specific types of social enterprises or social enterprise associations as needed.

- **Information gathering sessions with stakeholders:** In person or virtual meetings with stakeholders present an effective way to engage in comprehensive discussions with stakeholders. Though more time intensive than surveys, information gathering sessions may lead to greater insight into the specific needs and challenges of stakeholders.

- **Public commentary on proposed legislation:** Publishing proposed legislation to enable public feedback is an effective way to identify and address potential shortcomings before the legislation is formally adopted. One downside of this practice is that it may prevent stakeholders from participating in the development of the legal framework until a very late stage in the policy-making process.

- **Co-construction of legal frameworks** (see Box 2.7): Enabling stakeholders to participate in each stage of the legal framework development process helps to ensure that the legal framework is aligned with their broad needs and realities. This inclusive approach helps to facilitate broader acceptance of the legal framework and avoids excluding or constraining specific types of social enterprises. While effective, this approach can be time and resources intensive.

Lessons learnt

- **Top-down development of legal frameworks is very risky, though it may be convenient in the short run.** Top-down processes risks ignoring stakeholder needs and producing ineffective and potentially counterproductive legal frameworks.

- **Engaging with a diverse array of stakeholders helps develop legal frameworks that meet the real-world needs of social enterprises.** Identifying relevant stakeholders is important to ensure that all viewpoints are considered during the development of legal frameworks.

- **There are a number of ways to promote inclusion and obtain stakeholder inputs.** The best option is often context-dependent and reflects the specific priorities and constraints of a given policy-making process.

Step 7 - Regulating social enterprises: trends and options

What are the trends and options in recognising and regulating social enterprises?

Approaches to regulate specifically social enterprises

Social enterprises are either regulated through specific legal frameworks (e.g. France, Luxembourg, Italy, Slovenia) **or promoted through action plans and/or strategies** (e.g. Sweden, Australia). The European Comparative Synthesis Report on the social enterprise ecosystems (European Commission, 2020[2]) identifies three trends to regulate social enterprises:

- **The introduction of specific legal frameworks by adjusting existing cooperative or company legislation.** Specific social enterprise legislation most often derive from cooperative regulations, such as in France (collective interest cooperative society), in Italy (see Box 2.9) and Poland (social cooperative), or in Spain (social initiative cooperative). Company laws have been adjusted in the UK and in Latvia. Most of social enterprise legal forms across EU jurisdictions are adapted from the cooperative form because the latter is being perceived as a "natural dress" for social enterprises while an SE legal form adapted from the company form is perceived as having a weaker identity unless limits and clear rules are adopted on ownership and control (Fici, 2017[22]).

Box 2.9. Case study – Social Cooperatives Law in Italy: Adjustment of an existing cooperative law to support social enterprise development

In 1991, Italy established the Law 381/1991 on Social Cooperatives to legally recognise cooperatives that work with an explicit "aim to pursue the general interest of the community in the human promotion and social integration of citizens." The Law on Social Cooperatives was the first law to specifically recognise and regulate social enterprises in Italy. It has inspired similar laws across Europe and around the world in countries such as Portugal, France, Spain South Korea and the United States. Ever since, the Law on Social Cooperatives has seen several revisions and facilitated the development of legal frameworks for other areas of the social economy.

The Italian social cooperatives movement demonstrates how 'bottom-up' development of social and solidarity economy ecosystems can lead to the adoption of legal frameworks for social enterprises. In 1991, after almost ten years of unregulated development, the Italian Law recognised both new and existing social cooperatives and supported their expansion throughout Italy. According to the Italian National Institute of Statistics (ISTAT), before the inception of the Law on Social Cooperatives, there were around 2 000 social cooperatives which grew to 3 500 in the mid-nineties, to over 6 000 in 2003 and to over 11 000 social cooperatives as of 2011.

Italy demonstrates how a favourable and adaptive legal environment not only contributes to the steady development of social enterprises on a national level but can also serve as an inspiring model for other countries to create their own legal frameworks.

The complete case study available in Annex D further describes the legislation and its benefits to support the social enterprise development.

- The **introduction of new legal statuses that can be adopted by one or several legal forms**. The legal statuses can be adopted by diverse legal entities – for-profit and not-for-profit – provided that they meet certain criteria related to the social enterprise identity, regardless of the legal form in which they have been incorporated. An entity qualifies (and disqualifies) as a social enterprise depending on whether it complies with a minimum threshold of legal requirements. For example, Belgium, Denmark (see Box 2.10), Italy and Slovenia have introduced a social enterprise status accessible for one or several legal forms. The Belgian social enterprise legal status[5] is only available for cooperatives while the Italian social enterprise legal status[6] is available for commercial companies as well as for not-for-profit entities, such as associations and foundations. Some countries have introduced accreditation schemes for work integration social enterprises that can be adopted by a variety of legal forms (e.g. Poland, Slovenia and Spain). In Europe, the social enterprise legal status schemes correspond to a second wave of legislation and it is becoming the prevalent model (Fici, 2017[22]). The main advantage – even if there is no evidence so far that this is the most successful option – is the flexibility it provides as it allows a social enterprise to choose the legal form under which it prefers to conduct its business, according to the circumstances (e.g. the nature of the founders or members, first-degree social enterprise, etc.), the cultural and historical tradition where it has its roots (e.g. of associations or cooperatives), or the type of business to conduct (e.g. labour-intensive or capital-intensive) (Fici, 2017[22]).

Box 2.10. Case study – Registration tool for social enterprises: unleashing the potential of social enterprises through regulation in Denmark

In 2014, a registration tool for social enterprises (*Registreret Socialøkonomisk Virksomhed* – RSV) was introduced in Denmark under the National Strategy for Social Enterprise. This RSV tool, which is housed by the Danish Business Authority, presents a set of compliance criteria for social enterprises to be accredited by this voluntary legal status, such as inclusive governance and social management of profits, allowing for the recognition of businesses that operate with a social, occupational, health-related, environmental or cultural purpose. As of July 2021, 798 social enterprises were registered through the tool.

The RSV creates a common identity for social enterprises, increases their visibility and raises awareness and public trust around such enterprises in Denmark. The formal recognition provided by the tool allows for social enterprises to signal their social characteristics, and therefore facilitates access to potential customers, investors and partners, both in the public and private sector. Additionally, the RSV acts as a common database to collect information on social enterprises. Overall, the establishment of the registration tool has been an important step in the development of the social enterprise ecosystem in Denmark.

The complete case study available in Annex C further describes the features of the registration tool, its benefits to support the social enterprise development as well as the challenges still to be addressed.

- The **introduction of new legal statuses within a broader recognition of a larger field** – the social economy, the third sector or the social and solidarity economy – which formally recognises social enterprises as one dynamic among other social economy or third sector organisations and reinforces possible links with these actors. This recognition of a larger field includes either the adoption of a framework law on the social (and solidarity) economy (e.g. France, Spain), or the definition of the notion in a specific law, usually in laws that regulate social enterprises through a legal status (e.g. Luxembourg, Slovenia) (see Box 2.11). This last approach enables to regulate specific entrepreneurial forms – the social enterprises – while clearly integrating them in a wider set of organisations sharing common features and values.

Box 2.11. Defining the social (and solidarity) economy in legal frameworks

Two approaches – statutory and substantial – coexist to legally define the social (and solidarity) economy. The statutory approach consists of listing the legal forms that are part of the social and solidarity economy while the substantial approach defines the social and solidarity economy through a set of principles (Hiez, 2021[40]). Some countries, such as Luxembourg or Greece have adopted a substantial approach and define the guiding principles and values of the social and solidarity economy. Legal frameworks adopted in other countries, such as France, Portugal and Spain, provide a list of the legal forms being considered as part of the social and solidarity economy, relating to a statutory approach.

However, none of these countries follow a strict statutory approach as the legal frameworks also define the principles and common values of the social and solidarity economy, leaving a door open to other legal entities, when complying with these principles, to be recognised as part of the social and solidarity economy (Hiez, 2021[40]). As an example, the 2011 Law on the Social Economy in Spain defines the guiding principles of the social economy entities and lists the specific entities that

---

are included in the social economy. Likewise, the law opens to "those entities that carry out economic and entrepreneurial activity, whose operating rules comply with the principles listed in the previous article" (Article 5). The French and Portuguese laws adopt the same hybrid approach, recognising as part of the social and solidarity economy the entities that respect the guiding principles of the social economy defined in the legislation.

Legal forms and statuses used by *de facto* social enterprises

Social enterprises can take a diversity of legal forms and statuses that reflect entrepreneurial approaches within the social economy, including forms and statuses not specifically designed for them. Possible options include traditional legal forms adopted by social economy entities – such as the association, the cooperative, the foundation and the mutual society – as well as conventional enterprises provided that the legislations regulating these entities enable the introduction of specific requirements to align with the criteria defining social enterprises.

- **Non-profit legal forms** (e.g. foundations or associations) can be used by social enterprises provided that the legislation allows these entities to undertake economic and market-based activities, which is the case in Belgium, France Luxembourg and Slovenia for example. Denmark, Finland, Spain and Sweden on the contrary restrain the economic nature and market orientation of associations.

- **The cooperative legal form** can be used by social enterprises given that the legislation allows to benefit the general interest and address the needs of non-members, including vulnerable recipients, as it is the case in Slovenia and in Italy (social cooperatives) for example.

- Social enterprises can adopt the legal form of **a limited liability company** when legislations regulating these entities enable them to pursue a social purpose and/or to include restrictions to protect this social purpose (e.g. asset locks). The 2016 Luxembourg Law on Societal Impact Companies stipulates that as a departure from the provisions of article 1832 of the Civil Code, the incorporation act can mention that the company is not incorporated with the objective to provide a direct or indirect patrimonial benefit to the shareholders (Article 2). In Slovenia, legislation regulating limited liability companies provides for the introduction of specific constraints, such as the non-profit distribution constraint and the asset lock (OECD, 2022[41]; European Commission, 2019[42]).

- **Additional legal statuses** are also available for social enterprises, even if not designed specifically for them. This is the case of public benefit statuses that attach to organisations complying with certain criteria (e.g. Spain, France and Poland) and of Work Integration Social Enterprises (WISEs) as existing in many European countries.

Table 2.1. Approaches to regulate social enterprises

Different trends and options coexist to regulate the social enterprises. This matrix presents a comparison of legal approaches and the pros and cons of these options.

APPROACH	ADVANTAGES	CHALLENGES
Approaches to regulate specifically social enterprises		
Introduction of specific legal frameworks by adjusting existing cooperative or company legislations	• Provide social enterprises with a strong identity that relies on specific ownership and control rules	• Provide a less flexible approach • Do not enable to encompass pre-existing *de facto* social enterprises
Introduction of new legal statuses available for one or several legal forms	• Provide a flexible approach and enable entities to choose the most appropriate legal form under which it prefers to conduct its business • Provide a clear definition of social enterprises • Provide visibility and legal recognition to social enterprises	• May contribute to fragmentation and inconsistency among de jure and *de facto* social enterprises • Do not recognise social enterprises as part of a wider field, next to other social economy organisations • May need to be supported with fiscal incentives to unleash full potential
Introduction of new legal statuses within a broader recognition of a larger field – the social economy, the third sector or the social and solidarity economy	• Recognise and regulate social enterprises while clearly integrating them in a wider set of organisations sharing common features and values – the social economy field.	• May require awareness-raising, education and information to ensure clarity among different notions, such as social economy and social enterprise
Legal forms and statuses used by *de facto* social enterprises		
Non-profit legal forms (e.g. foundations or associations)	• The primacy of the social purpose is preserved thanks to the non-profit nature of these entities	• Legislation may prevent these entities from undertaking economic and market-based activities
Cooperative legal forms	• Provide a "natural dress" for social enterprises	• Legislation may prevent cooperatives from benefiting the general interest and addressing the needs of non-members
Limited liability company	• Provide an efficient tool to undertake economic activities	• May be perceived as having a weaker identity, possibly at risk unless limits and clear rules are adopted on ownership and control

Source: Authors' elaboration

Designing legal frameworks at the national and subnational level

Legal frameworks for social enterprises can be adopted at the national or at the subnational level, depending on the administrative organisation of the country. A national law can help reinforce the recognition of the social enterprises at a wider level and ensure coherence among diverse legal frameworks and support schemes while subnational legal frameworks can ensure a better alignment with local realities and needs and might be seen as an opportunity to experiment locally policy frameworks before deploying them to the whole country. However, multi-layered legislation may bring confusion, which might cause legal uncertainty and make social enterprises less attractive. But the coexistence does not necessarily bring confusion insofar as the field of application of each norm is clearly defined to avoid any contradictory provisions. In Belgium, the Brussels-Capital Region introduced in 2018 a specific "social enterprise" legal status available to all legal entities provided that they conform with a set of criteria; this regional legal status co-exists with the "social enterprise" legal status, only available for cooperatives, introduced at the federal level in 2019. The reflection around legal trends and options should also relate to what happens at the international as well as at the European level.

Box 2.12. Case Study: The Community Interest Company in the United Kingdom

Social enterprises in the UK can choose from a variety of legal forms, such as Community Benefit Society, Community Cooperative Society or Company Limited by Guarantee (CLG). However, the only legal form specifically designed to enable and regulate social enterprises is the Community Interest Company (CIC) that was introduced by the UK government as part of the 2004 Companies Act, following a range of consultations between the UK government and the social enterprise sector from 2002 to 2004. The CIC was established as a new type of limited company designed for social enterprises whose activities operate for the benefit of the community rather than for the benefit of the owners of the company. It is conceived as being flexible in terms of organisational structure (e.g. community co-operatives, single member companies) and governance arrangements (e.g. limited by guarantee, limited shares) while still providing limited liability.

The 2004 Companies Act also established the Office of the Regulator of CICs that is charged with deciding whether an organisation is eligible to become, or continue to be a CIC, as well as supporting the growth of CICs through "light touch regulation" and guidance on CIC matters. All CICs are required to deliver an annual report that is made available for the public. These reporting and disclosure requirements contribute to building perceptions of legitimacy of the CIC among the general public and potential investors.

The CIC form has been central to the development of the social enterprise sector in the UK, with just over 200 CICs registered in the first year (2005- 2006) and steadily growing to 18904 CICs in 2019-2020. Moreover, the introduction of CICs offered an important precedent for other, subsequent, developments of social enterprise organisational forms elsewhere. For example, the Canadian province of British Columbia introduced Community Contribution Companies (C3s) through amendment of their Business Corporations Act in 2012. In June 2016, Nova Scotia (Canada) passed the Community Interest Companies Act allowing a business to be designated as a Community Interest Company.

Source: (Office of the Regulator of Community Interest Companies, 2016[43]; Vincent, 2020[44]; Office of the Regulator of Community Interest Companies, 2016[45]; British Columbia Centre for Social Enterprise, 2014[46]; Canadian CED Network, 2016[47])

Lessons learnt

- The main purpose of adopting legal frameworks is to clearly define what a social enterprise and the type of support it is entitled to.
- The specific features of social enterprises related to governance and business models are translated into diverse criteria in legal frameworks.
- Different trends and options coexist to regulate the social enterprises. Understanding the pros and cons of these options is important to effectively regulate social enterprises.
- The reflection around legal trends and options should also relate to what happens at the international as well as at the European level.
- Creating a legal definition can help to grant tax incentives but a law is not always needed.

Step 8 - Leveraging fiscal policy for social enterprises

Creating a legal definition of social enterprises can help to allocate fiscal expenditures or grant tax incentives to them, but a law is not always needed. Fiscal instruments can stimulate social enterprise activity while driving positive social outcomes and saving public resources. It is important for policy makers to understand the potential of fiscal policy as an incentive to complement legal frameworks to support social enterprises as well as the array of fiscal instruments available to them. These tools represent an important way to support social enterprises even in the absence of a legal framework or specific legal status for social enterprises.

As elaborated in Table 2.2, target countries have granted social enterprises with a range of tax and fiscal benefits to promote their development. These mechanisms can be applied in a scaled manner based on the legal form of social enterprises or the criteria they should comply with as well as the level of commitment to social or public purposes. They can also reflect the unique conditions in a given country, region or city as well as specific objectives.

Although all target countries except for Denmark provide social enterprises with tax regime benefits depending on legal forms or legal status they adopt, most countries have not adopted specific laws providing fiscal benefits specifically targeted at social enterprises. The particular benefits are not linked to their particular status as a social enterprise but depend on the (i) legal form adopted by the entity and/or the (ii) activities that it is performing. Certain target countries such as Luxembourg, Poland, Slovakia, Slovenia, and Spain indicated the direct form of support, especially by provision of the grant, subsidies and state aid in different form and amount. Below is a summary of common fiscal tools:

- *Corporate tax exemptions*: In many target countries, social enterprises might be exempted from paying corporate tax on their profits, enjoy reduced VAT rates, or have social insurance costs reduced or covered by public subsidies.

- *Tax reimbursements*: These create tax incentives for individuals and businesses to donate to specific types of organisations that serve the public interest. In Italy and the Netherlands, individuals can donate to accredited organisations in order to win tax reimbursements, which helps facilitate access to finance for social enterprises and other social economy organisations. This approach can also extend to investors. In France and Italy, for example, investors in social enterprises are eligible for specific tax deductions.

- *Sector and activity specific benefits*: These benefits can be used to provide targeted support to specific sectors or types of legal forms. For example, Belgium provides social enterprises that operate within the health care and/or social service sectors with reduced social security tax rates. Likewise, France, Italy, Slovakia, and Slovenia provide specific incentives to social enterprises that create job opportunities for vulnerable or marginalised workers. These policies help to spur social enterprise activity within areas identified to be of particular importance to a given country, region or city.

- *Capital flow related tax benefits*. Countries could grant investors tax deductions on the capital invested into social enterprises. They can do so by reducing taxes on returns from financial investments in social enterprises. For example, in Italy, there are certain tax exemptions that apply to investors investing in non-profit limited companies or partnerships that pursue certain public benefits and qualify as "social enterprises." Investors are also allowed tax deductions on a portion of the capital that they have invested into such qualifying entities if they maintain their investments for five years (Bono, 2021[48]).

In **the Netherlands**, tax exemptions are the preferred option. Organisations that obtain PBO status are generally not subjected to the Dutch corporate income tax and can also obtain a VAT exemption. In **Spain**, social enterprises can benefit from lower tax rates compared to traditional firms, reduced social security contributions, and exemption on property tax. In **Italy**, all income earned by a social enterprise is not subject to tax, investors in social enterprises can deduct 30% of the amount granted for income tax purposes under certain conditions. Similarly, in **Poland** and **Slovakia,** social enterprises enjoy significant tax privileges such as tax exemptions (Poland) or reduced VAT for goods and services (Slovakia).

In **Belgium** the fiscal framework differs depending on the type of social enterprise, where associations and foundations can be taxed only on certain specific revenues and gains instead of application of standard corporate income tax; they can also benefit from the reduced VAT rate and social insurance costs; and further some of the donors (institutional or private) can be provided with tax reductions as well. As in Belgium, only certain types of companies (non-profit organisations and foundations) can benefit from the total exemption in **Luxembourg** (with exception of withholding tax and VAT).

Fiscal incentives represent an important tool to empower social enterprises to achieve their social missions while also saving public resources. Under certain conditions, social enterprises can support social welfare more effectively and at less cost than the public sector. Consequently, empowering social enterprises to expand their operations in these areas can drive social welfare benefits with little impact on public resources. For example, social cooperatives and other social economy organisations in Italy helped to fill gaps in existing public service provisions, particularly in rural areas. By creating a legal framework and developing favourable fiscal policies, Italy helped to drive social enterprise development and expansion and improve overall welfare while saving public resources.

Subnational governments that may lack the capacity to create new legal frameworks can leverage fiscal policy to support social enterprises within their jurisdiction. Even when developing legal frameworks for social enterprises is not an option, regional and local governments may leverage fiscal policy to stimulate social enterprise development.

In order to ensure efficiency of fiscal tools, countries often link tax benefits/exemptions to qualification criteria that identify social enterprises and reporting processes (e.g. Belgium). Reporting generally involves providing information about activities undertaken by the entity and the level of reporting that is required often correlates to the size of entity. For example, in Italy, social enterprises that are so-called "third sector" entities (i.e. operating in specific sectors such as health services, environmental safeguarding, scientific research, or humanitarian aid) with revenues greater than EUR 1 million per year must publish and file their social report with the national register of the third sector, in addition to publication on their website.

To help better targeting of benefits and simplification of tax policies, countries might consider setting up a specific body or task force within their tax authorities to grant and administer tax benefits to social enterprises, whether incorporated as for-profits or non-profits, and to audit eligible social enterprises to ensure compliance and prevent potential abuse (Bono, 2021[48]).

Table 2.2. Overview of fiscal benefits granted to social enterprises in the targeted EU countries

The table provides an overview of fiscal benefits for the social enterprises, at the national and subnational level, as well as other support mechanisms available. The table is not exhaustive due to the diversity of fiscal benefits and other support mechanisms that exist and that context-based.

	Fiscal benefits for social enterprises	Other support mechanisms
	EU Member States	
Belgium	• Under certain conditions, WISEs benefit from a reduced VAT rate. • Social security tax breaks are provided in the healthcare and social service sectors. • WISEs' profits put into an asset lock schemes are subject to tax reductions at the regional level. • Under certain conditions tax reductions for private and/or institutional donors can be provided.	• The Social Innovation Factory, created in 2013, "promotes, guides and supports social entrepreneurship and social innovation in tackling societal challenges" and combines the roles of advisory structure and incubator. • In Flanders, various measures were undertaken to support WISEs such a large structure for collective support programs, subsidies for management consultancy, support for innovation and CSR and scientific management courses. • Several social economy consulting agencies (Agences-conseil), which are recognised support and advice structures for social enterprises, currently operate in Wallonia.
Denmark	• Public benefit organisations do not pay any corporate income tax on their "ideal" activities nor on the economic activities necessary to support their social mission. • Organisations and social enterprises with the public-benefit status can use a reduced VAT rate of 7%, instead of the normal rate of 19%. • Social enterprises do not benefit from any exemption on indirect labour costs. If they have employees, they must follow all regulations.	• The Danish Centre for Voluntary Effort is a government-run centre that promotes the non-profit sector. • Many support mechanisms for the social enterprises were discontinued in 2015 due to shifting policy priorities at the national level.
France	• SCICs' revenue that is allocated to the asset lock is tax-exempt. • Sports and cultural associations can be exempt from corporation tax on services provided to their members. • Foundations are not subject to corporation tax for activities directly related to their purpose. • SCICs' VAT rate depends on the activity carried out. • Sporting and cultural associations can be exempt from VAT on services provided to their members. • Foundations are not subject to VAT for activities directly related to their purpose. • Associations and WISEs can benefit from reduced social security taxes for the employment of workers under certain conditions. • Legal entities can donate tax-free up to 10% of their previous year's profit or up to 3% of their personnel costs during the current year to eligible NPOs and foundations. • The total amount that individuals are allowed to deduct from their personal income is 1,200 EUR per year.	• Social economy enterprises have access to regional support schemes dedicated to innovation. • Associations are eligible for employment subsidies if they hire unemployed or low qualified workers. • All enterprises are eligible for public grants according to their activity field (social services, home care services, childcare, cultural activities, and sport, among others) • There are numerous although diversified support initiatives at regional level. Key initiatives include the Rhône-Alpes Forum of Solidarity Employment (until 2015) to promote employment in the sector, the PROGRESS program of the Provence-Côte d'Azur Region to develop the social economy, and the Languedoc-Roussillon Region initiative to provide support services to social innovation projects.
Italy	• Social cooperatives entities with SE status are exempted from payment of corporate tax (IRES). • A-Type social cooperatives enjoy a favourable (5%) VAT rate. • B-Type social cooperatives are exempt from the payment of social insurance contributions for the disadvantaged workers they have integrated. • Donating to public benefit organisations including social cooperatives qualifies donors for corporate tax advantages: a 20% reduction of the corporate tax	• The Marcora Fund facilitates access to finance for cooperatives. • The Ministry of Economic Development has actively supported social enterprises and social cooperatives since 2015.

	base for a single donation and an additional 20% reduction for a permanent donation contract. In addition, donations made by individuals are deductible from the personal income. • Donations of goods and services for public benefit purposes also receive VAT exemption. • Public benefit provisions govern non-profit companies if they have public benefit status. In this case, non-profit companies do not need to pay taxes after their public benefit activities and remain exempt from local business tax.	
Luxembourg	• SISs can benefit from exemptions from corporate income tax, communal business tax and net wealth tax. • Tax reductions granted to private and/or institutional donors exist but are not specified. • No legal provisions regarding exemption or reduced VAT rate for SISs.	• Department of Social and Solidarity Economy • 6zero1 is a government-run incubator supporting SISs. • SSE Cluster of the Greater Region is an initiative supporting SSE development in Luxembourg and the French region of Meurthe and Moselle.
Netherlands	• Corporate tax reduction for organisations meeting the requirements for public benefit status (ANBI status), such as having the aim and the actual activities of an organisation with 90% public interest. • Donations to organisations that have ANBI status can be deducted from income tax over and above a threshold of 1% of the total income reported to the tax authorities (and at least 60 EUR). The maximum deduction is 10% of this income.	• The municipality of Amsterdam has initiated a support program for WISEs which includes a variety of measures (e.g. investment fund, guidance, etc.). Another measure undertaken by the municipality is the "Project preparation Subsidy Sustainable Initiatives." • The municipality of Utrecht launched the "Working together for work" program as well as several platforms, such as the Social Impact Factory, in order to inform and connect social entrepreneurs.
Poland	• Some exemptions from income tax under certain conditions. • ZAZs and ENPOs are VAT exempt under certain conditions. • The employment costs of social cooperatives can be covered by a local government. If an ENPO acts as a CIS, it is allowed to benefit from a partial reimbursement of its employees' salaries. ZAZs' employment costs can be partially covered by PFRON.	• About 60 EU-funded social economy support centres provide business support services to SSE organisations and social enterprises.
Slovakia	• Civic associations and NPOs providing socially beneficial services and foundations are exempt from taxes for the non-profit activities. • VAT applies only in cases of SEs whose yearly taxable income is 50,000 EUR. • SEs with higher income registered according to the Act on Social Economy and Social Enterprises and those that are socialising 100% of their possible profit may apply for the lowered VAT rate. • In the case of employing a long-term unemployed person, the employer may apply for a reduced rate of social insurance payment. In case of employees with health disabilities, the health insurance payment is half that of other employees. • Tax percentage assignation model under which legal entities and natural persons may participate.	• All enterprises that create jobs for disadvantaged jobseekers can apply for a public subsidy supporting the newly created or sustained job. • A spectrum of financial aid schemes (investment and compensatory aid) has been introduced under Act on Social Economy and Social Enterprise.
Slovenia	• Associations, institutes, and foundations are exempt from paying taxes for non-profit activities. • Exemption from VAT for activities in the public interest and if taxable income does not exceed 50,000 EUR per year. • Companies and employment centres for people with disabilities are exempt from paying taxes and social security contributions for all employed persons in the company	• Most programmes, actions and tenders of the Ministry of Labour, Family, Social Affairs and Equal Opportunities are traditionally open to social enterprise organisation types in relation to active labour market policies, social affairs, family and people with disabilities. For instance, from 2009 to 2015 the Ministry allocated 8.3 million EUR to SE development, which included pilot project tenders and public works for SEs.

Spain	• Profits of social initiative cooperatives with a recognition of their non-profit mission can be exempt or applied to just 10% of revenues. Reduction of 95% in the Economic Activities Tax. • Special employment centres for social initiative can benefit from direct subsidy and reduction in the annual business tax for each people with disabilities hired. • Employment integration enterprises benefit from reductions in the social security contributions of workers at risk of exclusion. Subsidies for economic compensation of the labour costs supported due to the integration process. • Special employment centres not only those for social initiatives: benefit from reductions in the social security contributions of people with disabilities employed. Subsidies for economic compensation of the labour costs supported. • Donors (legal entities or physical persons) have no tax relief or other types of benefits.	• At the national level, three main measures have been developed to promote and support the social economy, in addition to the fiscal benefits: budget support (e.g. grants and subsidies for incorporating certain types of workers into the enterprises, direct investments in materials that contribute to the competitiveness of enterprises, subsidised technical support and training, etc.), technical assistance (e.g. providing support to SSE organisations in areas such as internationalisation or innovation), and employment policies (e.g. giving workers the possibility to capitalise unemployment benefits when the beneficiary decides to establish a cooperative).

Source: (European Commission, 2020[2]), 2020-2021 OECD focus groups

Lessons learnt

- **Fiscal policy can be used separately or in conjunction with legal frameworks to support social enterprises.**

- **Legal frameworks that do not leverage fiscal policy often lead to underused legal forms.** Creating tax incentives and developing fiscal instruments can promote uptake of new legal forms and drive engagement with social enterprises.

- **There is a diverse set of fiscal tools that can be utilised to support social enterprises or target certain outcomes.** Various combinations of available fiscal approaches and tax regimes can be used to meet local specificities and help address specific social, economic and environmental challenges.

Figure 2.6. Important steps for the development process

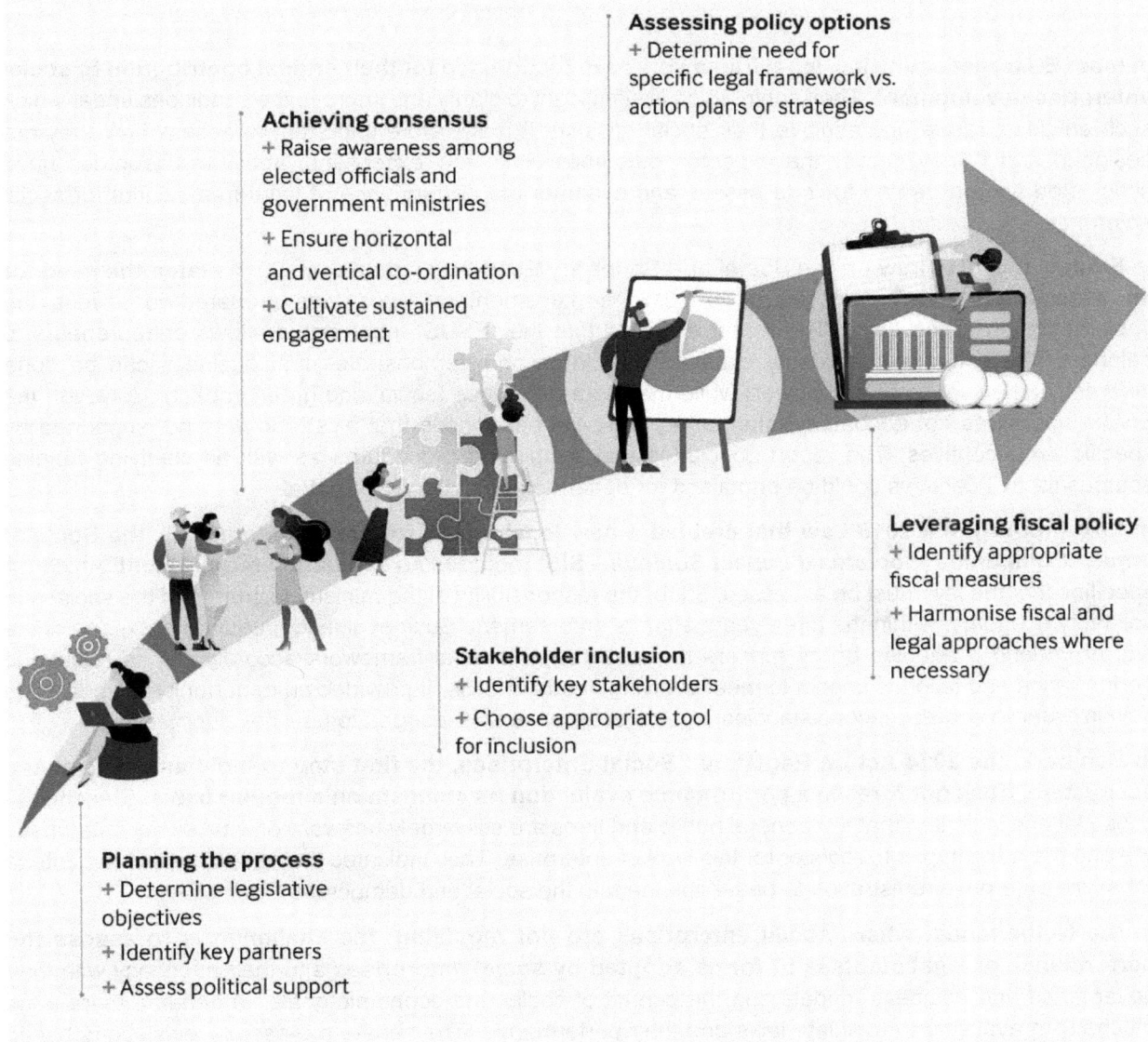

TOOLBOX
Navigating the legal framework development process

Assessing policy options
+ Determine need for specific legal framework vs. action plans or strategies

Achieving consensus
+ Raise awareness among elected officials and government ministries
+ Ensure horizontal and vertical co-ordination
+ Cultivate sustained engagement

Leveraging fiscal policy
+ Identify appropriate fiscal measures
+ Harmonise fiscal and legal approaches where necessary

Stakeholder inclusion
+ Identify key stakeholders
+ Choose appropriate tool for inclusion

Planning the process
+ Determine legislative objectives
+ Identify key partners
+ Assess political support

Source: Authors' elaboration

Evaluation phase: Assessing the performance of legal frameworks and adapting them to evolving needs

Step 9 - Assessing legal framework performance

Assessment of legal framework performance, a practice not widely anticipated

In most EU target countries, legal frameworks are recognised for their critical contribution to social enterprise development. Their contribution is significant to clarify and improve the conditions under which such entities operate and achieve their social mission. It is therefore important to assess how they are designed and if they deliver the expected outcomes. With few exceptions, not many countries have anticipated and/or created tools to assess and evaluate the performance of legal frameworks for social enterprises.

In France, the 2014 Law on the Social and Solidarity Economy, adopted in 2014 **stated the need for an assessment every two years**. In 2016, a parliamentary report was prepared to assess the implementation of the Law.[7] The report specifies that the "ESUS" legal status allows entrepreneurs to belong to the social and solidarity ecosystem at large and demonstrates that business can be done differently (share of profit and power) while making a difference (social and green impact). However, the ESUS label does not encompass the variety of social enterprises that exist and was not supported by specific tax incentives. The report concludes that simplifying procedures as well as clarifying funding sources/fiscal incentives could be prioritised for better uptake of the ESUS label.

In Luxembourg, the 2016 Law that created a new legal status for social enterprises, the Societal Impact Companies (*Sociétés d'Impact Sociétal* – SIS) includes an evaluation requirement. Article 15 specifies that the law must be assessed, under the responsibility of the ministry in charge of the social and solidarity economy, within the three years after its enforcement. Such evaluation requirement – one of the first of its kind – enables policy makers to recalibrate this legal framework according to its real-world performance and tailor its impact to meet evolving needs of SISs. It provides an opportunity to update the Law in order to address inconsistencies, ensure coherence and respond to new developments.

In Denmark, the 2014 Act on Registered Social Enterprises, the first step to build an entire policy ecosystem, does not foresee a performance evaluation mechanism on a regular basis. Stakeholder consultations indicated that the general public and firms are still largely unaware of what social enterprises are and the advantages to register for this type of enterprise. They indicated the need to revise the criteria for social enterprise registration to better link them to the social and democratic dimensions.

In the Netherlands, where social enterprises are not regulated, the challenge is to assess the performance of legal statuses or forms adopted by social enterprises and their adequacy with their governance and business models and the pursuit of social and economic goals. In general, there is no mechanism available to evaluate laws and their performance. The senate pre-assess legislations based on the criteria of effectiveness and simplicity which are common principles that need to be attended in laws.

In Slovakia, the Act 112/2018 on Social Economy and Social Enterprises states that there must be technical assistance to support its implementation but makes no reference to its performance evaluation or measurement of impacts. Stakeholder consultations indicated the need to develop capacity and allocate resources to conduct an evaluation process as well as to collect data to assess impacts of the law.

Box 2.13. Case study – Evaluation of Luxembourg Law on Societal Impact Companies

On 12 December 2016, Luxembourg adopted a law to regulate the creation of social enterprises under a new legal status: the Societal Impact Companies (*Sociétés d'Impact Sociétal* – SIS). The law not only defines principles of the social and solidarity economy (SSE), but also stipulates that the law must be assessed within three years after its enforcement.

This legal evaluation requirement – one of the first of its kind – enables policy makers to recalibrate a legal framework according to its real-world performance and tailor its impact to meet the ever-evolving needs of SISs. By engaging a variety of stakeholders in the two evaluations conducted since 2016, Luxembourg obtained input on how the legal framework was perceived on the ground and gathered feedback from those parties affected by it. To do so, the Luxembourg Ministry of Labour, Employment and Social and Solidarity Economy (MTEESSS) conducted consultations, including workshops, expert consultations, surveys, and a large-scale seminar with SSE crucial stakeholders.

As a result, amendments to the law that were adopted in 2018 resolved many of the residual uncertainties related to the transition of SSE organisations to the SIS regime. Specifically, this entailed amending existing legislation to extend specific rights such as tax exemptions to SISs that previously advantaged non-profit organisations and foundations. Consequently, the number of SISs increased: as of July 2019, there were 31 registered SISs, 25 of which obtained their accreditation after the 2018 amendment. The most recent amendment in 2021 took into account the unprecedented challenges SISs had to face during the COVID-19 pandemic, and addressed the need to reduce the administrative burden and to create incentives for more entrepreneurs to adopt the SIS accreditation.

The complete case study available in Annex E further describes the evaluation of the Luxembourg legal framework for social enterprises.

Improving legal frameworks through assessment of processes and outcomes

Assessment of legal framework performance usually covers two elements: i) *processes* and ii) *outcomes* (Box 2.14).

- *Processes* refer to how regulations are developed and enforced.
- *Outcomes* refer to whether legal frameworks have reached their objectives and their potential implications (positive and negative) on ecosystem development. This also helps determine the need for updates or revisions of laws.

Box 2.14. What is regulatory quality?

Pursuing "regulatory quality" is about enhancing the performance, cost-effectiveness, and legal quality of regulations and administrative formalities. The notion of regulatory quality covers **processes**, i.e. the way regulations are developed and enforced and their compliance with **the principles of consultation, transparency, accountability and evidence**. It also covers **outcomes**, i.e. whether regulations are **effective, efficient, coherent and simple**.

In practice, this means that laws and regulations should:

1. serve clearly identified policy goals, and are effective in achieving those goals;
2. be clear, simple, and practical for users;
3. have a sound legal and empirical basis,
4. be consistent with other regulations and policies;
5. produce benefits that justify costs, considering the distribution of effects across society and taking economic, environmental and social effects into account;
6. be implemented in a fair, transparent and proportionate way;
7. minimise costs and market distortions;
8. promote innovation through market incentives and goal-based approaches; and
9. be compatible as far as possible with competition, trade and investment facilitating principles at domestic and international levels.

Source: (OECD, 2012[49]; OECD, 2014[50])

Processes

To be successful legal frameworks for social enterprises need to be designed in an integrated approach with stakeholders. Processes of designing legal frameworks usually involve a wide range of stakeholders and institutions, also involved in their implementation. Some countries developed best practices (sometimes enshrined in the law itself) to ensure the design of legal frameworks for social enterprises are the outcome of co-construction processes involving networks and stakeholders across levels of government and sectors (Box 2.15).

> **Box 2.15. Examples of inclusive and open processes to legal frameworks for social enterprises**
>
> - **France**: Biennial consultations mobilising national and subnational authorities as well as representatives of the field have been introduced in the 2014 Law on the Social and Solidarity Economy, confirming a more bottom-up approach to building the ecosystem.
> - **Denmark**: A specific National Committee was created in order to prepare the Act of 2014.
> - **Slovakia**: A two year long consultation process was held during which inputs were collected from academics, social entrepreneurs and local governments, before adopting the Act on Social Economy and Social Enterprises in 2018.
> - **Spain**: A partnership model was developed to promote strong involvement of different stakeholders in processes pertaining to laws such the Law on the Social Economy in 2011 (Law 5/2011) which recognises the concept of social enterprise. The stakeholders include regional authorities, universities, associations, and the private sector (e.g. the Mondragon Cooperative Corporation) in addition to the Spanish Business Confederation of Social Economy (CEPES): an umbrella organisation created in 1992 to represent the companies of the social economy.
>
> Source: focus group discussions from target countries and beyond

The OECD 2012 Recommendation of the Council on Regulatory Policy and Governance and the 2014 Framework for Regulatory Policy Evaluation (OECD, 2014[50]) offer guidance on how countries can best use *consultation* to ensure legal and regulatory processes are inclusive and open to stakeholders. *Consultation* should ensure that legal and regulatory processes are open to interested groups and the public. Engaging all relevant stakeholders during the regulation-making process and designing consultation processes aims to maximise the collection of quality information and that needs as well as local practices of social enterprises are reflected and integrated in laws. A wide range of approaches could be used including informal consultation, circulation for comments, public hearings or creation of advisory bodies.

Figure 2.7. Phases and main steps of the consultation process

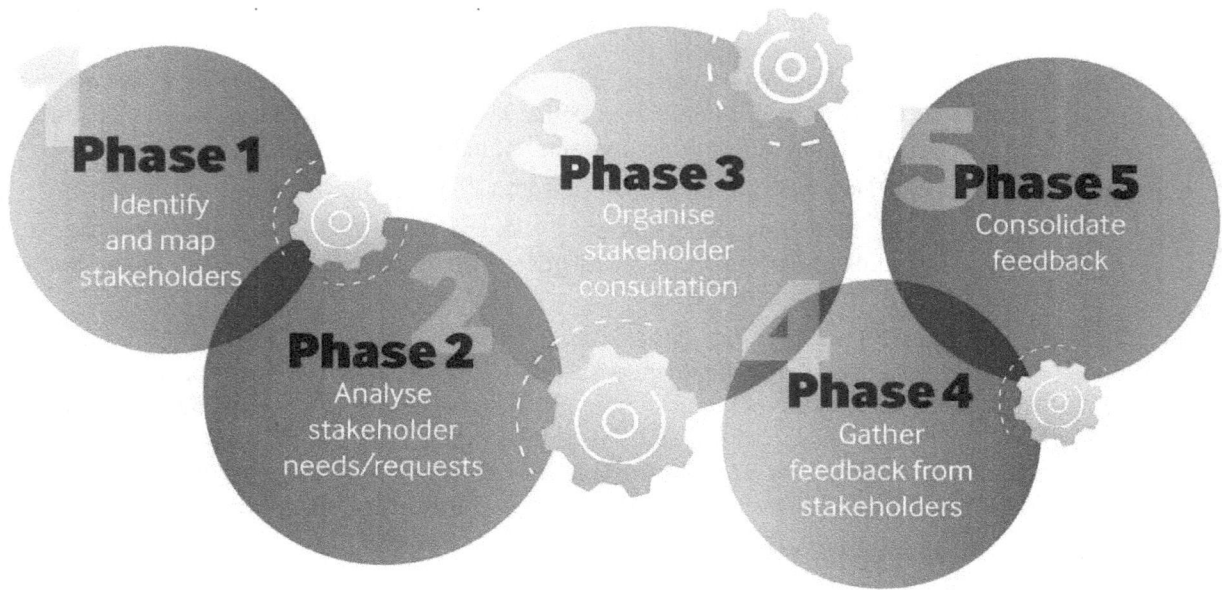

Source: Authors' elaboration based on OECD 2012 Recommendation of the Council on Regulatory Policy and Governance

The EU better regulation guidelines also set out principles on consultation to be used when preparing legal frameworks and when managing and evaluating legislation (Figure 2.8).

Figure 2.8. Phases and main steps of the consultation process

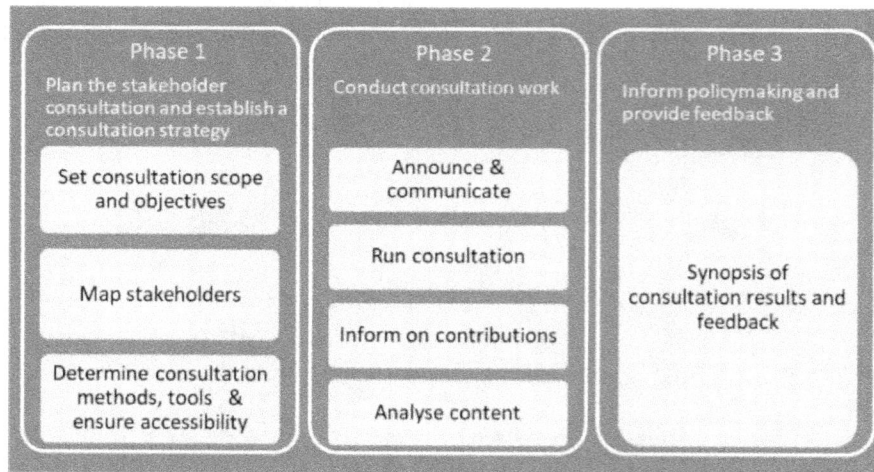

Source: (European Commission, 2021[51])

Outcomes

The performance of legal frameworks for social enterprises is strongly linked to their capacity to support the achievement of specific objectives: recognition, visibility, legal definitions, ease of registration, doing business, design of tailored taxation, etc. One indicator often used to assess the success or failure of legal framework outcomes is the share of entities that decide to register as social enterprises.

The number of newly registered social enterprises and the steady development of the field are clear indicators of positive legal framework performance, but they should not be the only criteria for assessments.[8]

Based on country-specific issues and the priorities that supported the introduction of laws, other criteria could/should be included. For example, the number of business closures (both traditional and social enterprises); the geography of social enterprises (urban/rural); the number and quality of jobs created and the contribution to the implementation of strategic priorities and policies. This could help better understand why some legal frameworks aren't appropriate in supporting social enterprises, and identify the unexpected consequences of regulations: more red tape, additional administrative burdens, heavy reporting procedures restrictions; complexity; lack of demand for legislation, poor knowledge of social enterprise needs. Strategies to assess the outcomes of legal frameworks for social enterprises should include end-users/ beneficiaries of regulation i.e. social enterprises themselves and/or their representatives. This could facilitate revisions and updates of laws when appropriate.

Regulatory Impact Analysis (RIA) is a tool that could support evaluation of outcomes of legal frameworks for social enterprises. RIA is a decision tool of (i) systematically and consistently examining potential impacts arising from government action and (ii) communicating the information to decision-makers. Legal frameworks are often designed with not enough knowledge of their consequences due to the lack of *ex-ante* assessment. This lack of understanding could lead to regulations being less effective, unnecessary and even burdensome. Therefore, Regulatory Impact Analysis applied to legal frameworks for social enterprises can be an effective strategy for improving their quality and ensuring that regulations are fit for purpose and will not cause more issues than they solve. The OECD developed a set of best practices for RIA that could inspire evaluation of outcomes of legal frameworks designed for social enterprises (Box 2.16).

Box 2.16. Regulatory Impact Analysis (RIA)'s Best Practices

1. Maximise political commitment to RIA

- Reform principles and the use of RIA should be endorsed at the highest levels of government. RIA should be supported by clear ministerial accountability for compliance.

2. Allocate responsibilities for RIA programme elements carefully

- Locating responsibility for RIA with regulators improves "ownership" and integration into decision-making. An oversight body is needed to monitor the RIA process and ensure consistency, credibility and quality. It needs adequate authority and skills to perform this function.

3. Train the regulators

- Ensure that formal, properly designed programmes exist to give regulators the skills required to do high quality RIA.

4. Use a consistent but flexible analytical method

- The benefit/cost principle should be adopted for all regulations, but analytical methods can vary as long as RIA identifies and weighs all significant positive and negative effects and integrates qualitative and quantitative analyses. Mandatory guidelines should be issued to maximise consistency.

---

5. Develop and implement data collection strategies

- Data quality is essential to useful analysis. An explicit policy should clarify quality standards for acceptable data and suggest strategies for collecting high quality data at minimum cost within time constraints.

6. Target RIA efforts

- Resources should be applied to those regulations where impacts are most significant and where the prospects are best for altering regulatory outcomes. RIA should be applied to all significant policy proposals, whether implemented by law, lower level rules or Ministerial actions.

7. Integrate RIA with the policy-making process, beginning as early as possible

- Regulators should see RIA insights as integral to policy decisions, rather than as an "add-on" requirement for external consumption.

8. Communicate the results

- Policy makers are rarely analysts. Results of RIA must be communicated clearly with concrete implications and options explicitly identified. The use of a common format aids effective communication.

9. Involve the public extensively

- Interest groups should be consulted widely and in a timely fashion. This is likely to mean a consultation process with a number of steps.

10. Apply RIA to existing as well as new regulation

RIA disciplines should also be applied to reviews of existing regulation.

Source: http://www.oecd.org/regreform/regulatory-policy/ria.htm

---

Step 10 - Adopting a dynamic perspective of legal frameworks

Another motivation to assess the performance of legal frameworks stems from the need to bring changes and amendments to adjust to emerging needs. Some provisions of legal frameworks tend to become obsolete over time or need to be updated/adjusted to bring parity with new social or economic situations/evolutions. Social enterprises and the markets in which they operate are inherently dynamic and have ever-evolving needs and challenges. For example, social enterprises are expected to play a greater role in crisis recovery and support the transition to more inclusive and greener economies and societies. As such, policy makers need to be prepared to adapt legal frameworks to new market developments and evolving stakeholder needs.

Stabilising the legal definition of the social enterprise would benefit policy efforts, aiming to clarify links with existing and emerging legal trends and concepts. This clarification is required to avoid the promotion of one concept – for example social enterprises – to the detriment of other concepts, for example within the social economy. New forms of purpose-led enterprises are constantly emerging. This reinforces the need to define the boundaries of social enterprises. Reducing legal uncertainty and possible overlaps among different legal concepts would ensure that policy support is targeted to help social enterprises expand without limiting the potential of other actors.

Legal frameworks that govern social enterprises should not be seen as static. It is important for policy makers to stay up to date with new developments in the social enterprise field in order to be prepared to adapt their approach to fit contemporary conditions as they emerge. Monitoring and evaluation activities that accommodate views across government ministries as well as from diverse stakeholders are critical in this respect. Evaluation can be used to adapt to emerging trends such as digitalisation and the effects of the ongoing COVID-19 crisis. Although OECD stakeholder consultations confirmed that policy makers in a number of target countries recognised the need to amend and/or update pre-existing legislation to support social enterprises, many also indicated that doing so was unlikely to take place in the near future due to insufficient cross-ministerial co-ordination, political commitment and expertise of social enterprises among policy makers. This common obstacle highlights the importance of regularly assessing the performance of legal frameworks and establishing effective and timely mechanisms to address underperforming or clashing legislation.

Political momentum needs to be sustained over time as challenges may emerge during the design and implementation of legal frameworks. Establishing a formal accountability mechanism such as the one developed by the Province of Quebec in Canada (see Box 2.17) can be a useful way to ensure the adaptability of legal frameworks over the long run while sustaining political momentum. Likewise, such mechanisms can help to link monitoring activities directly to policy actions that keep legal frameworks attuned to the real-world needs of social enterprises. Despite the benefits of monitoring and evaluation, few countries conduct *ex ante* or *ex post* evaluations of legal frameworks for social enterprises. The activities conduct as a result of such processes in Luxembourg testifies to the benefits of such approaches over time. Integrating such requirements helps to ensure that the necessary financial and human resources are available for future evaluations even if policy priorities have shifted towards new areas.

Box 2.17. The Accountability Mechanism of the Quebec Social Economy Act (Canada)

The Province of Quebec in Canada has adopted the Social Economy Act in 2013 with the objective to recognise the contribution of the social economy to the socioeconomic development and to sustain the government's commitment to the social economy in the long run.

The Act sets up an accountability mechanism to assess its outcomes. This accountability mechanism relies on three pillars:

- the establishment of a privileged relationship encouraging dialogue between the government and the social economy stakeholders, namely the *Chantier de l'économie sociale*, the *Conseil québécois de la coopération et de la mutualité* and the member-organisations of the Panel of Social Economy Partners;

- an obligation to adopt an action plan on the social economy, after consultation of the social economy stakeholders, every five years. The action plan also establishes the reporting mechanisms to account for the policy actions taken to support the social economy;

- a requirement to publish a report on the implementation of the action plan, which is also tabled in the National Assembly. The report serves, in combination with stakeholder consultations, as the basis to design the subsequent action plan.

In addition, a 10-year report is envisaged to assess the Social Economy Act and its long term effectiveness, with the objective of taking stock, reporting on changes having taken place, and adapting law to changing realities.

Source: Social Economy Act (Quebec, 2013), OECD stakeholder consultations, OECD international expert meeting on "Leveraging Legal Frameworks to Scale the Social and Solidarity Economy" (10 December 2020), (Quebec, 2020[52])

Figure 2.9. Legal framework performance evaluation checklist

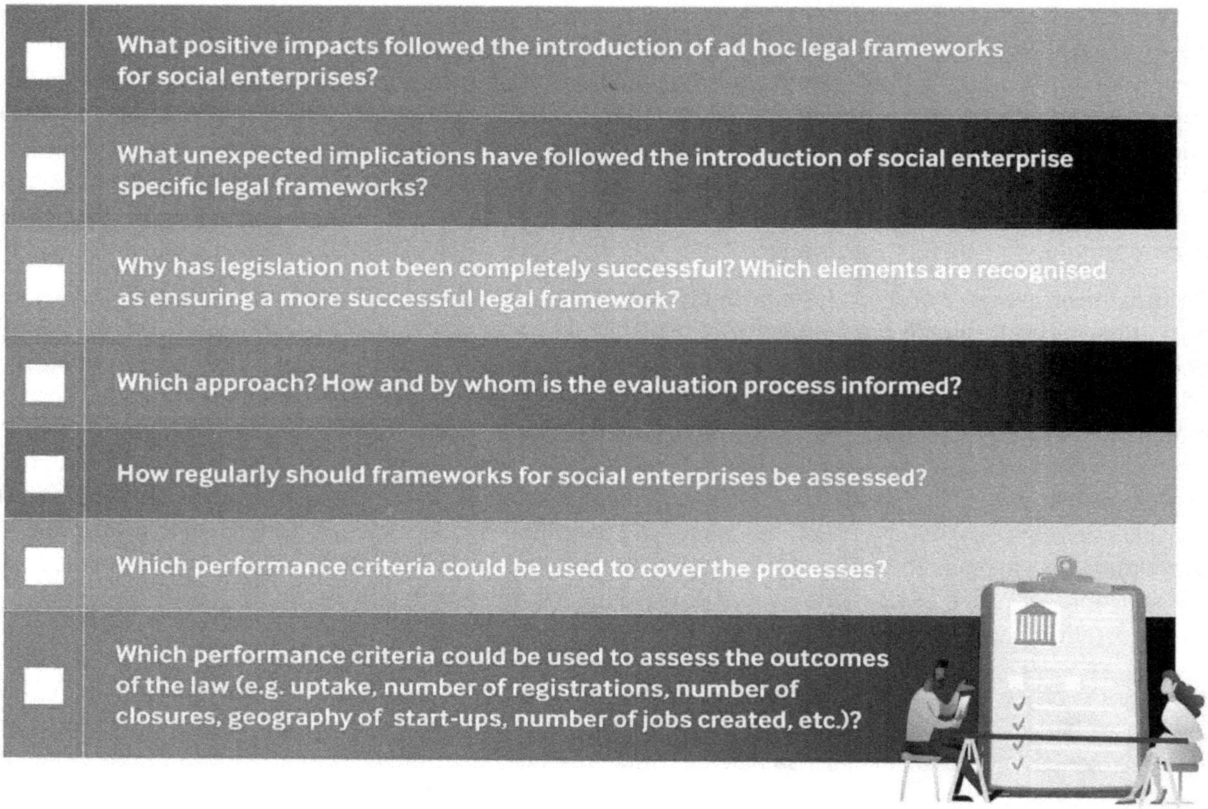

- What positive impacts followed the introduction of ad hoc legal frameworks for social enterprises?
- What unexpected implications have followed the introduction of social enterprise specific legal frameworks?
- Why has legislation not been completely successful? Which elements are recognised as ensuring a more successful legal framework?
- Which approach? How and by whom is the evaluation process informed?
- How regularly should frameworks for social enterprises be assessed?
- Which performance criteria could be used to cover the processes?
- Which performance criteria could be used to assess the outcomes of the law (e.g. uptake, number of registrations, number of closures, geography of start-ups, number of jobs created, etc.)?

Source: Authors' elaboration

Lessons learnt

- With the exception of France and Luxembourg which have included assessment requirements in the laws themselves, few countries conduct ex-ante or ex-post evaluation of legal frameworks for social enterprises and/or anticipate specific tools for their assessment.
- In countries where legal framework performance assessments were conducted, they helped ensure that regulation for social enterprises is:
  o easy to understand and use;
  o acceptable to stakeholders and ministries;
  o in line with international guidance (EU/OECD) and with international good practice;
  o legally and administratively feasible;
  o suitable for the development of social enterprises, established under different legal forms, with different business models, pursuing various social, societal or environmental missions;
  o compliant with the RIA rules for drafting legislation.
- Capitalising on the 2012 OECD Recommendation and Framework on Regulatory Policy and the EU better regulation guidelines, the following elements can be identified as critical to successful processes and outcomes:
  o a sequenced and inclusive process with clear preparatory steps for consultation and with an active involvement of relevant stakeholders;
  o peer learning to identify best practice of stakeholder engagement and dialogue in similar contexts;
  o data, capacity and resources to ensure feasibility and effectiveness of performance assessment;
  o a set of clear and context-based criteria to conduct assessment of outcomes of legal frameworks:
    – the share of *de jure* and *de facto* social enterprises,
    – the number of newly registered social enterprises where there is a registry;
    – the number of closures;
    – the geography of social enterprises (urban/rural);
    – the number and quality of jobs created by social enterprises
    – sectors and activities of social enterprises;
    – their contribution to the implementation of strategic priorities and policies.
  o periodicity to define when assessment and evaluation could take place. This could be achieved through annual conferences that bring together all the stakeholders of the ecosystem to achieve greater consensus;
  o regular adjustments and revisions in consultation with stakeholders to adapt legal frameworks to new developments within markets and evolving stakeholder needs.

Figure 2.10. Important criteria for evaluation

TOOLBOX
Evaluating legal framework performance

Context-based criteria

+ Share of de jure and de facto social enterprises

+ Number of newly registered social enterprises where there is a registry

+ Number of closures

+ Geography of social enterprises (urban/rural)

+ Number and quality of jobs created by social enterprises

+ Sectors and activities of social enterprises

+ Contribution to the implementation of strategic priorities and policies

Processes

+ Sequenced and inclusive process with clear preparatory steps for consultation and with an active involvement of relevant stakeholders

+ Peer learning to identify best practice of stakeholder engagement and dialogue in similar contexts

+ Data, capacity and resources to ensure feasibility and effectiveness

Outcomes

+ Easy to understand and use

+ Acceptable to stakeholders and ministries

+ In line with international guidance (EU/OECD) and with international good practice

+ Legally and administratively feasible

+ Suitable for the development of social enterprises, established under different legal forms, with different business models, pursuing various social, societal or environmental missions

+ Compliant with the RIA rules for drafting legislation

References

Amsterdam Impact (2017), *Social Entrepreneurship Action Programme: Progress Report*.　　[33]

Barraket, J. et al. (2017), "Classifying social enterprise models in Australia", *Social Enterprise Journal*, Vol. 13/4, pp. 345-361.　　[12]

Barraket, J., C. Mason and B. Blain (2016), *Finding Australia's Social Enterprise Sector 2016. Final Report*.　　[13]

Bono, L. (2021), *Legal reform as a catalyst for social enterprise*, https://www.lexmundiprobono.org/wp-content/uploads/2022/01/Lex_Mundi_ProBono_A4_Report_INTERACTIVE_2022.pdf.　　[48]

Borzaga, C. and J. Defourny (2001), *The Emergence of Social Enterprise*, Routledge.　　[18]

Borzaga, C. and G. Tallarini (2021), *Social Enterprises and COVID-19: Navigating Between Difficulty and Resilience*, https://doi.org/10.5947/jeod.2021.004.　　[8]

British Columbia Centre for Social Enterprise (2014), *Community Contribution Companies (C3)*.　　[46]

British Council (2020), *Innovation and resilience: a global snapshot of social enterprise responses to COVID-19*, https://www.britishcouncil.org/society/social-enterprise/news-events/reports-social-enterprises-higher-education-country-reports.　　[9]

Caire, G. and W. Tadjudje (2019), "Towards a Global Legal Culture of the SSE Enterprise? An International Comparison of SSE Legislation", *RECMA*, Vol. 2019/3/353, pp. 74-88.　　[19]

Canadian CED Network (2016), *Community Interest Companies Now Availalbe in Nova Scotia*, https://ccednet-rcdec.ca/en/new-in-ced/2016/06/17/community-interest-companies-now-available-nova.　　[47]

Christiaan de Brauw, Allen & Overy (2020), *The Dutch Stakeholder Experience*, https://corpgov.law.harvard.edu/2020/08/02/the-dutch-stakeholder-experience/.　　[30]

CIRIEC (2017), *Recent evolutions of the Social Economy in the European Union*, http://www.ciriec.uliege.be/wp-content/uploads/2017/10/RecentEvolutionsSEinEU_Study2017.pdf.　　[1]

European Commission (2021), *Better Regulation Guidelines*, https://ec.europa.eu/info/sites/default/files/swd2021_305_en.pdf.　　[51]

European Commission (2020), *Social enterprises and their ecosystems in Europe Country Report Poland*, https://ec.europa.eu/social/BlobServlet?docId=22455&langId=en.　　[21]

European Commission (2020), *Social enterprises and their ecosystems in Europe. Comparative synthesis report*, Publications Office of the European Union, https://ec.europa.eu/social/main.jsp?catId=738&langId=en&pubId=8274.　　[2]

European Commission (2020), *Social enterprises and their ecosystems in Europe. Country Report Spain*, https://europa.eu/!Qq64ny.　　[27]

European Commission (2020), *Social enterprises and their ecosystems in Europe. Updated country report: Italy*, Publications Office of the European Union, https://europa.eu/!Qq64ny.　　[28]

62 |

European Commission (2020), *Social enterprises and their ecosystems in Europe. Updated country report: Luxembourg*, Publications Office of the European Union, https://europa.eu/!Qq64ny. [20]

European Commission (2020), *Social enterprises and their ecosystems in Europe. Updated country report: Poland*, https://europa.eu/!Qq64ny. [34]

European Commission (2020), *Social enterprises and their ecosystems in Europe. Updated country report: Slovakia*, Publications Office of the European Union, https://europa.eu/!Qq64ny. [26]

European Commission (2020), *Social enterprises and their ecosystems in Europe. Updated report France*, https://europa.eu/!Qq64ny. [24]

European Commission (2019), *Social enterprises and their ecosystems in Europe. Updated country report: Denmark*, Publications Office of the European Union, http://Available at https://europa.eu/!Qq64ny. [25]

European Commission (2019), *Social enterprises and their ecosystems in Europe. Updated country report: Slovenia*, Publications Office of the European Union, Luxembourg, https://europa.eu/!Qq64ny (accessed on 22 June 2021). [42]

European Commission (2019), *Social enterprises and their ecosystems in Europe. Updated country report: The Netherlands*, Publications Office of the European Union. [29]

European Commission (2011), *Social Business Initiative. Creating a favourable climate for social enterprises, key stakeholders in the social economy and innovation*. [16]

European Union (2021), *Regulation 2021/1057 of the European Parliament and of the Council of 24 June 2021 establishing the European Social Fund plus (ESF+) and repealing regulation 1296/2013*. [17]

Fici, A. (2017), *A European Statute for Social and Solidarity-Based Enterprise*, European Union. [22]

Government of Ireland (2019), *National Social Enterprise Policy for Ireland 2010-2022*, https://s3-eu-west-1.amazonaws.com/govieassets/19332/2fae274a44904593abba864427718a46.pdf. [35]

Hernández Salazar, G. and A. Olaya Pardo (2018), "El marco legislativo y su efecto sobre el crecimiento del sector cooperativo en Colombia (1933-2014)", *REVESCO. Revista de Estudios Cooperativos*, Vol. 127, pp. 139–158, https://doi.org/10.5209/reve.58398. [38]

Hiez, D. (2021), *Guide pour la rédaction d'un droit de l'économie sociale et solidaire*, ESS Forum International. [40]

International Labour Office (ILO) (2019), *Financial Mechanisms for Innovative Social and Solidarity Economy Ecosystems*, https://www.ilo.org/global/topics/cooperatives/publications/WCMS_728367/lang--en/index.htm (accessed on 4 March 2022). [39]

Lalor, T. and G. Doyle (2021), *Research on Legal Form for Social Enterprises*, https://rethinkireland.ie/wp-content/uploads/2021/12/Research-on-Legal-Form-for-Social-Enterprises.pdf. [36]

OECD (2022), "Boosting social entrepreneurship and social enterprise development in Slovenia: In-depth policy review", *OECD Local Economic and Employment Development (LEED) Papers* 2022/02, https://doi.org/10.1787/8ea2b761-en. [41]

OECD (2020), "Regional Strategies for the Social Economy: Examples from France, Spain, Sweden and Poland", *OECD Local Economic and Employment Development (LEED) Papers*, No. 2020/03, OECD Publishing, Paris, https://doi.org/10.1787/76995b39-en. [4]

OECD (2020), *Social economy and the COVID-19 crisis: current and future roles*, OECD Publishing. [11]

OECD (2019), "Boosting social entrepreneurship and social enterprise development in the Netherlands: In-depth policy review", *OECD Local Economic and Employment Development (LEED) Papers*, No. 2019/01, OECD Publishing, Paris, https://doi.org/10.1787/4e8501b8-en. [31]

OECD (2018), *Job Creation and Local Economic Development 2018. Preparing for the Future of Work*, OECD Publishing, https://doi.org/10.1787/9789264305342-en. [6]

OECD (2014), *Framework for Regulatory Policy Evaluation*, https://doi.org/10.1787/9789264214453-en. [50]

OECD (2013), *Policy Brief on Social Entrepreneurship*, OECD, https://www.oecd-ilibrary.org/industry-and-services/boosting-social-entrepreneurship-and-social-enterprise-development-in-the-netherlands_4e8501b8-en. [3]

OECD (2012), *Recommendation of the Council on Regulatory Policy and Governance*, https://www.oecd.org/governance/regulatory-policy/2012-recommendation.htm. [49]

OECD (2009), *The Changing Boundaries of Social Enterprises*, Local Economic and Employment Development (LEED), OECD Publishing, Paris, https://doi.org/10.1787/9789264055513-en. [23]

OECD (1999), *Social enterprises*, OECD Publishing. [15]

OECD/European Commission (2022), *Making the Most of the Social Economy's Contribution to the Circular Economy*, forthcoming. [5]

Oetelmans, E. (2015), *Actieprogramma Sociaal odernemen 2015-2018*, https://assets.amsterdam.nl/publish/pages/867586/actieprogrammasociaalondernemenamsterdam_2015-2018_2.pdf. [32]

Office of the Regulator of Community Interest Companies (2016), *Department for Business, Energy and Industrial Strategy, Information Pack*, https://assets.publishing.service.gov.uk/government/uploads/system/uploads/attachment_data/file/605429/13-783-community-interest-companies-information-pack.pdf. [43]

Office of the Regulator of Community Interest Companies (2016), *Information and Guidance Notes: Chapter 8: Statutory Obligations*, https://assets.publishing.service.gov.uk/government/uploads/system/uploads/attachment_data/file/605420/13-711-community-interest-companies-guidance-chapters-8-statutory-obligationstions.pdf. [45]

Quebec (2020), *Application de la loi sur l'économie sociale. Rapport 2013-2020.* [52]

Queensland Government Department of Employment, S. (n.d.), [14]
https://desbt.qld.gov.au/training/future-skills-fund/social-enterprise-grants.

Social Enterprise UK (2021), *No Going Back: State of Social Enterprise Survey 2021*, [10]
https://knowledgecentre.euclidnetwork.eu/2022/01/12/european-social-enterprise-monitor-report-2020-2021-2/.

Social Enterprise UK (2018), *Hidden Revolution. Size and Scale of Social Enterprise in 2018*. [7]

Thomson Reuters Foundation and Mason Hayes & Curran LLP (2020), *Social Enterprises in Ireland. Legal Structures Guide*, https://www.socent.ie/wp-content/uploads/2020/11/Social-Enterprises-In-Ireland-TrustLaw-Guide-November-2020.pdf. [37]

Vincent, A. (2020), *The Regulator's Community Interest Companies (CIC) Annual Report 2019 to 2020*, https://communityinterestcompanies.blog.gov.uk/2020/09/09/annual-report-2019-to-2020-community-interest-companies/. [44]

Notes

[1] The social economy refers to the set of associations, cooperatives, mutual organisations, foundations and social enterprises, whose activity is driven by values of solidarity, the primacy of people over capital, and democratic and participative governance (OECD, 2018[6]). Social enterprises distinguish themselves from social economy organisations by a more pronounced entrepreneurial and often innovative approach - their source of income coming primarily from commercial activities, rather than grants and donations (OECD, 2018[6]).

[2] Focus group discussion Italy, 18 December 2020.

[3] Social cooperatives; entrepreneurial non-profit organisations (ENPOs); professional activity establishments (ZAZs); and non-profit companies.

[4] A working definition is usually introduced in/by a policy document such as a national action plan or a strategy.

[5] See Code des sociétés et des associations (revised in 2019).

[6] See Legislative Decree 112/2017. It is also relevant to note that social cooperatives and their consortia acquire by law the qualification of Social Enterprise according to the new legal framework under Legislative Decree 112/2017.

[7] N° 3557 - Rapport d'information de MM. Yves Blein et Daniel Fasquelle déposé en application de l'article 145-7 alinéa 1 du règlement, par la commission des affaires économiques sur la mise en application de la loi n°2014-856 du 31 juillet 2014 relative à l'économie sociale et solidaire (assemblee-nationale.fr).

[8] (2020) OECD Highlights -Webinar "Leveraging Legal Frameworks to Scale the Social and Solidarity Economy".

Annex A. Data collection – Expert meetings and interviews

This annex provides the list of institutions and organisations involved in the expert meetings and in the interviews conducted by the OECD in the framework of this Action.

Expert meetings	
Belgium	Work And Social Economy Department, Flanders Region
	Office Of The Minister Bernard Clerfayt, Brussels-Capital Region
	Economy And Employment, Brussels Regional Public Service
	Tax Institute, University Of Liege
	Sociale Innovatie Fabriek
	Febecoop
	W.Alter, Sowecsom (Sriw)
	Concertes (2 representatives)
	Impact Advocaten
Denmark	Social Entrepreneurs Denmark
	Foldschack, Forchhammer, Dahlager & Barfod
	Selveje Denmark
	Social Responsibility and SDGs, Danish Business Authority
	Roskilde University (2 representatives)
	Kooperationen
France	Groupe Up
	Ecofi
	Alcya Conseil
	Université De Franche-Comté
	Région Nouvelle-Aquitaine-RTES
	Groupe Bpce - Chambre Francaise De L'ESS
	Université Paris-Est Créteil
Italy	Università di Trento
	Politecnico di Milano, School of Management
	Università degli Studi di Roma – Tor Vergata
	Forum del Terzo Settore (2 representatives)
	Università degli Studi del Molise
	ANCI Emilia Romagna
	ConfCooperative
	LUISS University
	REVES
	Federsolidarietà Lombardia
	RP Legal & Tax
	Fondazione ASM Brescia

Luxembourg	6zero1 Sa Sis Et Maison De L'économie Sociale Et Solidaire
	Département de l'Economie Sociale et Solidaire, Ministère du Travail, de l'Emploi et de l'Economie Sociale et Solidaire
	Université de Luxembourg
	Ecotransfaire/Le Cluster Économie Sociale Et Solidaire Grande Région (2 representatives)
	Cell – Transition Hub Luxembourg
The Netherlands	Nyenrode Business University
	Code Sociale Ondernemingen
	Tax Manager Knowledge Centre, PwC Netherlands
	Utrecht University School of Law
	Erasmus University Rotterdam
	Van Doorne N.V.
Poland	Ministry Of Finance
	Legal expert
	Public Procurement Law Centre For Private Governance (Cepri) and Faculty Of Law, University Of Copenhagen
Slovakia	Comenius University
	Ministry of the Interior of the Slovak Republic, Plenipotentiary of Slovak Government for Roma communities (2 representatives)
	Alliance for Social Economy in Slovakia
	ASSE - Association of subjects of social economy (2 representatives)
	Alliance for Social Economy in Slovakia
	Centre of Social and Psychological Sciences of Slovak Academy of Sciences
Spain	Director General Acción Exterior - Region of Navarra
	Expert -SOKIO COOP (SDAD. COOP. AND.)
	Valencia University
	CEPES
	EMES Network
	Spanish Cooperative Federation
	Mondragon Corporation
	Department of Business Management, University of Zaragoza

Interviews

Mouves (France)

LEST-CNRS, Université Aix-Marseille (France)

ULESS (Luxembourg)

Brussels Region (Cabinet Trachte) (Belgium)

PREMIKI (Slovenia)

3lobit (Slovakia)

Utrecht University School of Economics (The Netherlands)

Social enterprise expert (Slovakia)

Social Enterprise NL (The Netherlands)

Ministerie van Economische Zaken en Klimaat (The Netherlands)

Annex B. Case study – The Brussels 2018 Ordinance on social enterprises (Belgium): An inclusive policy-making process to co-construct a legal framework for social enterprises

What

Based on the EMES International Research Network approach of the social enterprise, the 2018 Ordinance establishes a set of criteria organised in three dimensions – social, economic and governance – and defines 'social enterprise' as private or public legal entities that implement an economic project, pursue a social purpose, and exercise democratic governance. In addition, the legal framework sets out the public support schemes that social enterprises can leverage, including financial and non-financial assistance.

The Ordinance on the accreditation and support of social enterprises was adopted on 23 July 2018 in the Brussels-Capital Region in Belgium. The adoption of this Ordinance results from a two-year consultation process with various stakeholders, including the Economic and Social Council of the Brussels-Capital Region (CESRBC), the Brussels Employment Office Actiris, the Brussels Social Economy Consultation Platform extended to ConcertES[1] and SAW-B (see the steps below). Additional stakeholders, such as academics, federations of social enterprises and social enterprises themselves, also participated in the consultation process, especially to establish the definition of the social enterprise.

Why

When designing legal frameworks, an inclusive consultation process may be of fundamental importance as it refines how policy makers understand social enterprises and thus ensures that legal frameworks are relevant, appropriate and meet the needs of relevant stakeholders. Finally, co-constructing a legal framework helps avert practical implementation problems, enhances compliance and acceptance of such framework, and increases public trust in government.

Until recently, social enterprises and the social economy in the Brussels-Capital Region were largely associated with the work integration field. The objective of this policy-making process was twofold: (1) the revision of the 2004[2] and 2012[3] Ordinances on the social economy and the accreditation of work integration social enterprises; and (2) the recognition of social enterprises beyond the work integration field. Adopting a co-construction approach allowed the Government of the Brussels-Capital Region to collect valuable information from a variety of stakeholders to better capture the situation experienced by work integration social enterprises but also to refine their understating of the needs and realities of social enterprises working on issues beyond work integration.

Key Activities

The 2018 Brussels Ordinance on social enterprises results from a thorough and inclusive co-construction process between employer's representatives, trade unions, social enterprise community, academics, and policy makers. The policy-making process to develop this legal framework took place over a period of two years and went through a range of crucial steps. In December 2016, the Office of the Brussels Minister of Employment and Economy (Minister's Office) drafted a political note for the ordinance project in collaboration with the Brussels Economy and Employment Administration (BEE). This note was then presented to the Social Economy Consultation Platform as well as social economy experts including ConcertES. In March 2017, the note was approved by the Government of the Region. In parallel to this process, the Minister's Office asked the CESRBC, the Social Economy Consultation Platform and Actiris to share their opinions on the note. These three organisations submitted their recommendations by September 2017.

Main steps of the policy-making process of the Brussels 2018 Ordinance on social enterprises

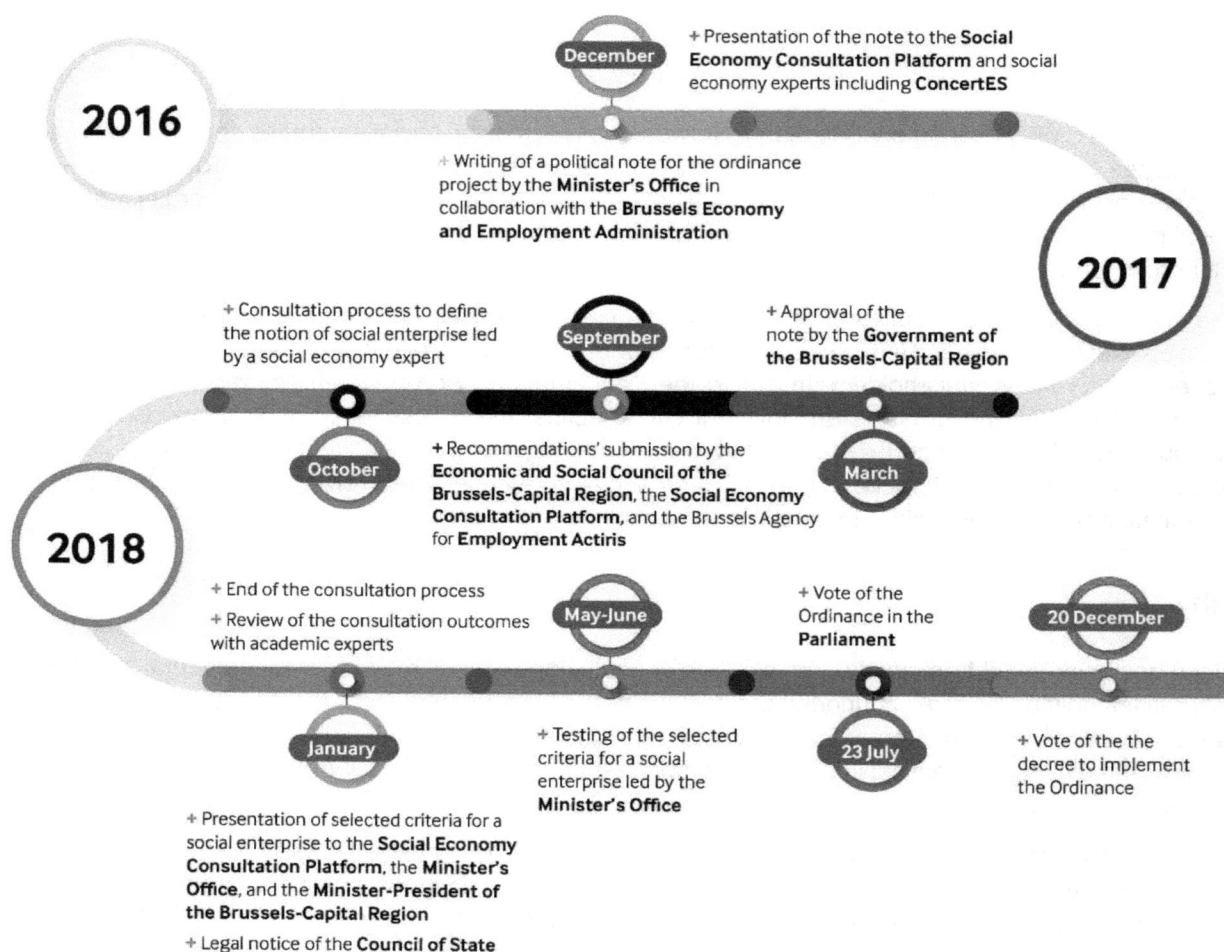

2016

December
+ Presentation of the note to the **Social Economy Consultation Platform** and social economy experts including **ConcertES**

+ Writing of a political note for the ordinance project by the **Minister's Office** in collaboration with the **Brussels Economy and Employment Administration**

2017

+ Consultation process to define the notion of social enterprise led by a social economy expert

September

+ Approval of the note by the **Government of the Brussels-Capital Region**

October
+ Recommendations' submission by the **Economic and Social Council of the Brussels-Capital Region**, the **Social Economy Consultation Platform**, and the Brussels Agency for **Employment Actiris**

March

2018

+ End of the consultation process
+ Review of the consultation outcomes with academic experts

May-June

+ Vote of the Ordinance in the **Parliament**

20 December

January

+ Testing of the selected criteria for a social enterprise led by the **Minister's Office**

23 July

+ Vote of the the decree to implement the Ordinance

+ Presentation of selected criteria for a social enterprise to the **Social Economy Consultation Platform**, the **Minister's Office**, and the **Minister-President of the Brussels-Capital Region**
+ Legal notice of the **Council of State**

Source: Authors' elaboration

The next step was to define social enterprises and to establish the criteria to recognise the entities covered by the legal framework. Given the complexity of defining social enterprises, the Minister's Office appointed a social economy expert to determine a set of criteria for a social enterprise. Starting from October 2017, the expert led a four-month consultation process which brought together federations and representatives of the social economy (e.g. Febisp, FeBIO, Tracé Brussel and SAW-B). More precisely, the expert conducted individual interviews with main actors in the field and organised three working groups to discuss the pre-defined criteria. The first one was composed of work integration social enterprises, the second one of social enterprises that did not focus on work integration, and the third one of social economy public institutions (*Institutions publiques d'Economie sociale* – IPES). The Minister's Office did not directly partake in the consultation but organised regular meetings with the social economy expert in order to follow the advancement of the process.

In January 2018, after reviewing the consultation outcomes with academic experts, the selected criteria defining a social enterprise were presented to the Social Economy Consultation Platform, the Minister's Office, and the Minister-President of the Brussels-Capital Region. Additionally, upon request of the Council of State, a test run of these selected criteria was conducted with main actors in the field in May and June 2018. To do so, the BEE shared a survey with all structures already recognised by the former scheme for work integration enterprises as well as with other social enterprises.

Based on the survey results, the criteria for a social enterprise were included in the draft ordinance and the decree to implement the ordinance. The draft ordinance was then examined by the Committee on Economic Affairs and Employment of the Brussels Parliament in July 2018 and was voted in the Parliament on 23 July. Finally, the decree to implement the Ordinance was passed on 20 December 2018. As of June 2021, 155 social enterprises were accredited in the Brussels-Capital Region.

Impact

By starting the consultation process at an early stage of policy development, the Government of the Brussels-Capital Region helped maximise the value of stakeholder engagement. Engaging with a broad range of actors allowed to design a legal framework that is more aligned with the field's needs and realities and that reflects a range of views in a proportionate way, thus avoiding its anchoring in a single ideology of social entrepreneurship. Such an inclusive policy-making process has also facilitated a broader acceptation of the criteria for social enterprises and enabled a common understanding and interpretation of the legal framework. Ultimately, the process has fostered dialogue between policy makers and main actors in the field. The dialogue remains open today and allows to easily gather these main actors around a table when needed.

The 2018 Ordinance had a positive impact on social enterprises as it has strengthened their legal certainty in relation to European State Aid legislation and has thus increased their access to financial resources. It has also allowed social enterprises to improve their internal processes, in particular regarding their governance. In short, the Brussels Ordinance on social enterprises and its policy-making process helped to both build common understanding of social enterprises and structure the overall field, which in turn fostered the development of social enterprises in the Brussels-Capital Region.

Table A B.1. List of main stakeholders involved in the policy-making process of the Brussels 2018 Ordinance on social enterprises

Stakeholder	Description
Actiris	Actiris is the Brussels Employment Office. As such it is tasked with implementing Brussels employment policy and ensuring the proper functioning of the job market in the Brussels-Capital Region. To this end, Actiris provides a wide range of services to businesses and jobseekers.
Brussels Economy and Employment Administration (BEE)	Brussels Economy and Employment contributes to the development of employment and supports the social economy. In this respect, it assumes many roles such as the approval and financing of social enterprises. BEE also promotes the socio-professional integration of workers who are particularly far from the labour market.
ConcertES	ConcertES is the concertation platform for organisations representative of the social economy active in the French-speaking part of Belgium.
Economic and Social Council of the Brussels-Capital Region (Conseil économique et social de la Région de Bruxelles-Capital - CESRBC)	CESRBC is the Region's main consultative body on socioeconomic matters. It brings together the social partners: organisations representing employers, the self-employed, the non-profit sector and employees.
FeBIO	FeBIO (Federatie van Brusselse Initiatieven ter Ontwikkeling van de Werkgelegenheid) is the Dutch-speaking federation of social integration enterprises in Brussels.
FeBISP	FeBISP is the Brussels Federation of Socio-Professional Integration and Social Economy Integration Organisations. It is currently composed of 79 structures and 97 projects active in these two sectors.
Government of the Brussels-Capital Region	The Government of the Region is the executive body of the Brussels-Capital Region.
Parliament of the Brussels-Capital Region	The Parliament of the Brussels-Capital Region prepares the texts, votes the budgets and controls the regional Government.
Social Economy Consultation Platform (Plateforme de concertation de l'Economie Sociale)	This Platform gathers representatives of the Government of the Brussels-Capital Region, the Administration of Economy and Employment of the Ministry of the Region and the Brussels Regional Employment Office, as well as representative organisations of employers in the social economy sector, and of workers and employers sitting on the Economic and Social Council of the Brussels-Capital Region.
Solidarité des Alternatives Wallones et Bruxelloises (SAW-B)	SAW-B is a federation of social economy actors, as well as a research and training centre, offering integrated support to social enterprises and shaping, through lobbying activities, an institutional landscape favourable to their development. SAW-B notably co-ordinates CoopCity, Brussels centre dedicated to social, collaborative and cooperative entrepreneurship.
Tracé Brussel	Tracé Brussel is a Dutch-speaking organisation that tackles unemployment in Brussels. Its mission is to strengthen the position of all job-seekers on the labour market, especially vulnerable groups, and to promote their integration. Together with a network of partners, Tracé Brussel develops innovative paths towards training, employment and an inclusive economy.

References

- Borzaga, C. and J. Defourny (2001), *The Emergence of Social Enterprise*, Routledge.
- Government of Belgium (n.d.), Ordonnance relative à l'agrément et au soutien des entreprises sociales. http://www.ejustice.just.fgov.be/eli/ordonnance/2018/07/23/2018031816/justel.
- OECD (2019), Better Regulation Practices across the European Union, OECD Publishing, Paris. https://doi.org/10.1787/9789264311732-en.
- Plateforme de Concertation de l'Economie Sociale (2017). Avis concernant l'avant-projet d'ordonnance relative à l'agrément et au soutien de l'entrepreneuriat social.
- SAW-B (2017). Réforme de l'ordonnance bruxelloise: se donner les moyens de ses ambitions.
- Zwarts, P. (2019). Inspirations et contingences dans la politique économique bruxelloise en matière d'entreprises sociales. En référence à l'ordonnance de 2018, Université catholique de Louvain.

Notes

[1] The Brussels Social Economy Consultation Platform gathers representatives of the Government of the Brussels-Capital Region, the Administration of Economy and Employment, and the Brussels Regional Employment Office, as well as representative organisations of employers in the social economy sector, and of workers and employers sitting on the Economic and Social Council of the Brussels-Capital Region. ConcertES was invited to join the process as it is the concertation platform for the organisations representative of the social economy active in the French-speaking part of Belgium.

[2] *Ordonnance relative à l'agrément et au financement des initiatives locales de développement de l'emploi et des entreprises d'insertion.*

[3] *Ordonnance relative à l'économie sociale et à l'agrément des entreprises d'insertion et des initiatives locales de développement de l'emploi en vue de l'octroi de subventions.* This 2012 Ordinance was never put into force, due to the lack of applicable decrees. The 2004 Ordinance was therefore the only one used as a reference before the 2018 Ordinance.

Annex C. Case study – Registration tool for social enterprises: Unleashing the potential of social enterprises through regulation in Denmark

What

The registration tool for social enterprises – *Registreret Socialøkonomisk Virksomhed (RSV)* – was introduced in Denmark under the National Strategy for Social Enterprise (2014 Act on Registered Social Enterprises (Act 711/2014)) and is run by the Danish Business Authority. All legal forms with limited liability[1] are eligible to be accredited by this voluntary legal status if they comply with a specific set of criteria. These criteria require that: the purpose of the enterprises is social and concerns social, employment, health, environmental or cultural aims; a significant share of revenues is generated through sales of goods and services; both the management and operations are independent from the public sector; governance is inclusive and allows stakeholder involvement; and the profit generated is reinvested to support the social mission (a maximum of 35% of after-tax profits can be distributed to owners and investors).

The Registered Social Enterprises tool provides a platform for social enterprises to register upon submission of a set of documents to prove that the social enterprises meet the register's admission criteria. The tool requires registered social enterprises (referred to as the "socio-economic enterprises" in the registry) to keep the documents up to date, as a compliance measure. Additionally, the registered social enterprises must report specific information in their annual report or appendixes (e.g. remunerations received by the company's management, founders and owners; description of the implementation of the social purpose criterion, the inclusive and responsible management criterion and the independence of the public sector criterion). Additionally, the enterprises can de-register at any point and are legally obliged to do so if the enterprise no longer meets the registration criteria. As of 5 July 2021, 798 social enterprises had registered through the RSV tool.

Why

The Registered Social Enterprises (RSV) Tool is part of a comprehensive national policy framework adopted in 2014 to support social enterprise development. Both the 2014 Act on Registered Social Enterprises and the registration tool it established create a common identity for social enterprises in the country. They enhance the visibility and development of the social enterprises that meet the criteria and enable data collection on the social enterprise ecosystem in Denmark. By registering, social enterprises signal their social characteristics to the public and private sectors and to the individuals. Registration facilitates their positioning as natural partners for collaboration with the public sector and potentially helps them to get a greater access to potential customers, investors and partners and increases public trust in the social enterprise ecosystem.

Key activities

At the local level, several municipalities (such as Copenhagen, Silkeborg, Ikast-Brande and Jammerbugt) do advertise the register and have created local support systems for social enterprises, serving as an evidence of the significance of the RSV Tool in developing the social enterprise ecosystem through a bottom-up approach. Recently, the project "*Rummelig Genstart*" was launched by *Projekter Imidt* and *Kooperationen*, a cooperative employer's organisation, with the support of the Danish Programme for the European Social Fund, to mitigate the negative effects from the COVID-19 crisis as well as to promote inclusion in the labour market. The objective is to create commercial partnerships between social and conventional enterprises. Social enterprises allowed to apply to this project should either be a registered social enterprise, a social enterprise in the process of registration, or an organisation that has a non-profit purpose and work with a social and economic bottom line. In this way, the project works to incentivise social enterprises to formally register.

Impact

In 2018, the Danish Business Authority, in consultation with stakeholders, evaluated the Act on Registered Social Enterprises and the registration tool – as scheduled in the preparatory work of the Act. The evaluation was conducted to assess whether the registration system had contributed to the formation of a common identity. At that time, 283 entities had registered as socio-economic enterprises, 173 of which were established after the act came into force in 2015. This early development stage is reflected in the data on employment as well, with 50% of registered socio-economic enterprises having no paid employment, 17% employing one person and only 33% employing two persons or more. Over two thirds of registered socio-economic enterprises (71%) are active in two industries namely, culture, leisure and other services (117) and public administration, education and health (84). The most frequently used legal forms included associations (43%) and limited liability companies (30%). Supplementing this data with qualitative analysis, the agency conducted interviews with both registered socio-economic enterprises and those that had deregistered.

The study concluded that the scheme could be improved to reach the objective to raise awareness around social enterprises as originally intended by the act. One of the main challenges was the lack of awareness of the register among eligible organisations, partly explaining the limited number of entities that had so far been included in the register. While the registry has not reached its full potential, in particular given the change in political context, it is nonetheless a crucial step towards creating a coherent approach to institutional and legal frameworks to support the social enterprise ecosystem, as it was advocated by the Committee on Social Economy, an informal working group with high-level stakeholders that emerged in an effort to sustain the policy initiatives already in place. The barriers to success of this regulation could be addressed by implementing the policy recommendations set out by this Committee, namely to provide guidance, fiscal and financial incentives, training opportunities and support for public procurement upon registration in order to strengthen the uptake of the legal status.

Despite these challenges, the number of registrations has been growing, from 283 in 2018 (across Denmark, however, most voluntary organisations are located in Copenhagen and Aarhus) to 620 in 2020 and 798 in July 2021, notably thanks to an increased interest at the local level.

References/further information

- https://www.retsinformation.dk/eli/lta/2014/711
- https://socialeentreprenorer.dk/registreringsordningen-for-socialoekonomiske-virksomheder/
- https://erhvervsstyrelsen.dk/vejledning-registrering-som-registreret-socialoekonomisk-virksomhed

- https://erhvervsstyrelsen.dk/sites/default/files/2019-03/evaluering_af_lov_om_registrerede_socialoekonomiske_virksomheder.pdf
- Sørensen, Katja Isa, and Anker Brink Lund. "Komparative analyser af dansk socialøkonomi."
- Hulgård, Lars, and Lisa Maurer Chodorkoff. Social Enterprises and their Ecosystems in Europe: Country report, Denmark. European Commission, 2019.

Note

[1] Legal forms include: Public limited company (Aktieselskab – A/S), Private limited company (Anpartsselskab – ApS), Limited partnership company (Partnerselskab – P/S), Entrepreneurial limited company (Iværksætterselskab – IVS), Limited liability cooperative society (Andelsselskab med begrænset ansvar – A.m.b.A), General partnership (Interessentskab – I/S), Limited partnership (kommanditselskab – K/S), Commercial foundation (Erhvervsdrivende fond – ERF), and Limited liability association (Forening med begrænset ansvar – F.m.b.A). For more information see: https://socialeentreprenorer.dk/registreringsordningen-for-socialoekonomiske-virksomheder/. Translations in English are based on: https://www.ecb.europa.eu/stats/money/aggregates/anacredit/shared/pdf/List_of_legal_forms.xlsx.

Annex D. Case study – Law on Social Cooperatives in Italy: Adjustment of an existing cooperative law to support social enterprise development

What

In 1991, Italy established the Law 381/1991 on Social Cooperatives to legally recognise cooperatives that work with an explicit "*aim to pursue the general interest of the community in the human promotion and social integration of citizens.*" The law regulates two types of social cooperative forms:

- A-type, i.e. social cooperatives providing social welfare or educational services; and
- B-type, i.e. social cooperatives integrating vulnerable or disadvantaged individuals into work through agricultural, manufacturing or other commercial activities. B-type social cooperatives should include at least 30% 'disadvantaged workers' among their workforce for whom they are exempted from social security contributions.

The Law 381/1991 on Social Cooperatives is a pioneering legal framework, as it was the first law to specifically recognise and regulate social enterprises in Italy. It has inspired similar laws in Europe and globally such as in Portugal, France, Spain South Korea and the United States. Ever since, the Law on Social Cooperatives has seen several revisions and facilitated the development for legal frameworks for other areas of the social economy.

Why

Social cooperatives are prominent drivers of welfare provision, and have seen an annual growth rate of 10% to 20% since their inception in the late 1960s and early 1970s when welfare gaps emerged as certain social needs were not adequately met be either the public or private sectors in Italy. The inability of the Italian welfare state to meet new needs arising primarily from demographic transformations, economic recession, and increasing unemployment prompted the citizen-led development of cooperatives and other types of social economy organisations, allowing them to complement the social services provided by the public authorities or address gaps in the Italian social welfare systems. The steady development of the social cooperatives catalysed the adoption of a new legal framework to recognise and support their action. The development of social enterprises, largely in the form of social cooperatives, began comparatively earlier in Italy than in most European member states, such as Portugal which adopted a Law-Decree on social solidarity in 1998. In 1991, after almost ten years of unregulated development, the Italian Law recognised both new and existing social cooperatives and supported their expansion throughout Italy.

An important accelerator for social cooperative development in Italy was the removal of the Crispi Law in 1988. The Crispi Law (6972/1890) stated that the responsibility of providing welfare services is limited to public entities or to the citizens themselves. However, the Constitutional Court ruling 396 of 1988 declared the Crispi Law unconstitutional, expanding the provision of welfare services to private entities. This ruling enabled cooperatives to legally promote the general interest while engaging in economic activity. It enabled them to act as social enterprises in addition to pursue the mutual interest of their members. This contributed to the promotion of the social enterprises and the third sector in Italy.

Key activities

The Italian social cooperatives movement is a demonstration of how 'bottom-up' development of social and solidarity economy ecosystems can lead to the implementation of specific legal frameworks for social enterprises. Post World War II, the cooperative movement gained momentum and relevance in Italy, leading to the recognition of its "social function" in article 45 of the Constitution of the Italian Republic. A group of volunteers began the Italian social cooperatives' movement with an aim to create stable and financially sustainable enterprises under the 'social solidarity cooperatives' banner that would be independent from volatile public and private funding mechanisms. The efforts of the voluntary groups led to an increasing demand for the social services provided by social cooperatives and progressively attracted public resources. This contributed to the development of legal frameworks for the social cooperatives.

The development of Law on Social Cooperatives predated additional legal frameworks to regulate social enterprises. Law 118/2005 and Legislative Decree 155/2006 recognise social enterprises through a legal status,[1] allowing for a wide range of entities (associations, foundations, religious institutions, cooperatives, limited liability and shareholder companies) to conduct economic activities with a social purpose, thereby increasing their share contributed to the GDP of the Italian economy.

Despite Law 118/2005, the number of registered social enterprises did not increase significantly due to the lack of fiscal incentives for registered social enterprises[2] and the additional costs in qualifying as social enterprises. Moreover, the number of social cooperatives did not increase either, as the Law 106/2016 reforming the "third sector" requires the existing social cooperatives to register and modify their status in order to comply with the new regulations. These barriers to the growth both in size and number of the social enterprises led to the emergence of the 2016/2017 legislation that expands on the existing framework for social enterprises with the objectives of reforming the third sector while conforming to the European Union's operational definition of social enterprises.[3]

Impact

According to Italian National Institute of Statistics (ISTAT), before the inception of the social cooperatives law, there were around 2 000 social cooperatives which grew to 3 500 in the mid-nineties, to over 6 000 in 2003 and to over 11 000 social cooperatives as of 2011. In 2015, the number of social cooperatives reached 59 027, accounting for 1.3% to the total share of the companies operating in Italy and employing over 1.1 million people, representing 7.1% of the total employment within the private sector. Cooperatives[4] also generated 4% of the value added (VA) of the private sector estimated at EUR 28.6 billion in 2015.

The 1991 Law on Social Cooperatives also resulted in the recognition of social cooperatives as providers of social services and increased their visibility, creating new markets for social services. The Law allowed for public-private partnerships in the provision of welfare services by clarifying the modalities of work with social cooperatives for public authorities. It has enabled a steady development of the third sector and the inception of legal frameworks for multiple legal forms of social enterprises in Italy, such as associations, foundations, and shareholder companies, among others.

The Italian Law 381/1991 on Social Cooperatives is the first generation of laws developed to specifically regulate social enterprises, acting as a cornerstone legislation in the promotion of social and solidarity economy ecosystems across Europe in Portugal, Spain, Greece, France, Hungary, Czech Republic and beyond in the United States. This Law provided a model of legislation for social enterprises at the European

Union level and at a Global level, leading to the replication and use of A-Type and B-Type form of social enterprises as defined by the Law such as in South Korea.

References

- Borzaga, C., et al. "Social enterprises and their ecosystems in Europe." Comparative synthesis report. Luxembourg, LU: Publications Office of the European Union (2020).
- Borzaga, C., et al. "Structure and performance of Italian cooperatives: a quantitative analysis based on combined use of official data." Journal of Entrepreneurial and Organizational Diversity 8.1 (2019).
- Fici, Antonio. "Recognition and Legal Forms of Social Enterprise in Europe: A Critical Analysis from a Comparative Law Perspective, Euricse Working Papers, n. 82/15." (2015): 1-29.
- Fici, Antonio. "A European Statute for Social and Solidarity-Based Enterprise." Policy Department C: Citizens' Rights and Constitutional Affairs, European Union (2017).
- Gonzales, Vanna. "Italian social cooperatives and the development of civic capacity: a case of cooperative renewal?" Affinities: A Journal of Radical Theory, Culture, and Action (2010).

Notes

[1] The Law 118/2005 legally recognises as "social enterprise" any organisations that qualify the following criteria: it is a private legal entity; it engages in the regular production and exchange of goods and services having "social utility" (i.e. it engages in one or more of the entitled sectors specified by the same law) and seeking to achieve a public benefit purpose rather than to generate a profit. An organisation is considered a social enterprise if it generates at least 70% of its income from entrepreneurial activities (i.e. production and exchange of goods and services having social utility); it is allowed to make a profit, but it cannot distribute it to its members or owners (non-distribution constraint). All profits have to be reinvested to further its main statutory (public benefit) goal or to increase its assets, which are fully locked; it is registered in the Social Enterprise Section of the Register of Enterprises managed by the Chamber of Commerce; and it publishes both its financial and social balance sheets.

[2] At the time, social enterprises regulated by the Legislative Decree 155/2006 were bound to the payment of corporate tax, VAT, IRAP and social security costs if they engaged in work integration activities. Conversely, social cooperatives benefited from an exemption from corporate tax on restrained profits and tax exemption on donations, as well as from a 4% VAT rate for A-type social cooperatives and an exemption from social security contributions for the disadvantaged workers for B-type social cooperatives.

[3] EU operational definition—a social enterprise is now defined as a "private organisation that runs entrepreneurial activities for civic, solidarity and social utility purposes and allocates profits principally to achieve its corporate purpose by adopting responsible and transparent management modalities and favouring the largest possible participation of employees, users, and other stakeholders interested in its activities".

[4] Excluding credit and insurance companies.

Annex E. Case study – The 2016 Law on Societal Impact Companies in Luxembourg

What

In December 2016, Luxembourg adopted a law to regulate the creation of social enterprises under a new legal status: the Societal Impact Companies (*Sociétés d'Impact Sociétal* – SIS). The law defines the social and solidarity economy (SSE) as a "mode of doing business" performed private legal persons that cumulatively meet the following four conditions: 1) distribution or exchange of goods or services; 2) supporting vulnerable groups or contributing to social and societal objectives through their activity; 3) autonomous management; 4) the reinvestment of at least half of profits in the company's activity. Additionally, this law provides that any legal entity (e.g. public limited company, limited liability company, cooperative company) complying with these SSE principles may opt for the SIS status.

One of the main characteristics of this law is its evaluation requirement. Article 15 stipulates that the law must be assessed within three years after its enforcement, by the Minister in charge of the SSE. This evaluation requirement – one of the first of its kind – enables policy makers to recalibrate this legal framework according to its real-world performance and tailor its impact to meet the ever-evolving needs of SISs. It provides them an opportunity to update the 2016 Law in order to address inconsistencies, ensure coherence and respond to new developments.

Why

The evaluation of a legal framework after its implementation — also referred to as *ex post* evaluation — uses evidence to assess whether such framework achieved its desired objectives, to better understand the mechanisms by which it produced the expected outcomes, and to identify unintended effects. This evaluation is crucial to revise a legal framework and ensure it remains effective, efficient and coherent over time.

In Luxembourg, this evidence-based assessment was first conducted through a variety of stakeholder and expert consultations, giving them an opportunity to provide feedback on the 2016 Law. Such process helped improve the legal framework according to SSE actors' demands, inform other SSE related laws and foster collective learning.

It is commonly acknowledged that the 2016 Law on Societal Impact Companies has considerably changed the legal environment in which social enterprises can operate. It has contributed to facilitate their establishment, as well as to increase their visibility and credibility. Additionally, many stakeholders agree that, by defining the criteria for the SSE, the law has been an important milestone towards better recognition of the SSE and all its actors in Luxembourg.

Key Activities

In the first semester of 2017, the Luxembourg Ministry of Labour, Employment and Social and Solidarity Economy (MTEESSS) launched a consultation process with other ministerial departments to determine the scope of legislative provisions that could be amended to ensure that social economy organisations that opt for the SIS status are not penalised. Additionally, the Social and Solidarity Economy Union of Luxembourg (*Union Luxembourgeoise de l'Économie Sociale et Solidaire* – ULESS) brought forward several proposals for legislative changes to the MTEESS in October 2017.

In March 2018, the MTEESS initiated consultations with Ministries to precisely identify aid and contracting systems with non-profits and foundations in the SSE sector that would require an adaptation of the legislative provisions in force. As a result, the Law of August 31, 2018 on SIS, amending many legislative provisions applicable to SSE companies, was adopted. This new legislation aimed at extending explicit rights to SISs that previously advantaged non-profit organisations and foundations, such as tax exemptions. According to ULESS, the amendment resolved many of the residual uncertainties related to the transition of SSE enterprises incorporated primarily as non-profits or foundations to the SIS regime.

In May 2020, the MTEESS started to conduct an analysis of the effects of the law since its enforcement. To do so, the MTESS conducted several consultations during the year, including workshops, expert consultations, surveys to SISs, and a large-scale seminar with SSE crucial stakeholders. These consultations highlighted a need to reduce the administrative burden, in particular for small entities that lack resources, and to create incentives for more entrepreneurs to adopt the SIS accreditation. In order to address these issues and taking into account the unprecedented challenges SISs had to face during the COVID-19 pandemic, another amendment was adopted in summer 2021

In short, engaging stakeholders in the ex-post evaluations was particularly useful to obtain input on how the legal framework was perceived on the ground and to gather feedback from those parties affected by it. The inputs allowed to improve the law through amendments, which made the SIS accreditation more attractive to SSE entities.

Impact

The MTEESS involved a wide range of stakeholders during its consultation processes including the Luxembourg ministries, the ULESS, SISs, SSE experts and critical actors. Such processes allowed to gather significant insights on challenges faced by SISs and discuss potential legislative adjustments to remove them.

The ULESS considers that the amendment of the 2016 Law in 2018, following the first evaluation, truly advanced legal security for all SSE enterprises and established SISs as an important enabler of social economy development. Moreover, it contributed to increasing the number of SISs. In fact, as of July 2019, there are 31 registered SISs, 25 of which obtained their accreditation after the 2018 amendment.

While the law of 12 December 2016 could be considered as a first legislative recognition of the social and solidarity economy in Luxembourg, the law of 31 August 2018 consolidated the SSI as the go-to legal form for enterprises operating in the social economy.

References

- European Commission (2017), EU Better Regulation Toolbox, https://ec.europa.eu/info/betterregulation-toolbox_en.
- European Commission (2020), A map of social enterprises and their eco-systems in Europe - Country Report:
- Luxembourg, https://www.euricse.eu/social-enterprises-and-their-ecosystems-in-europemapping-study/.

- Gouvernement du Grand-Duché de Luxembourg (2016), *Loi du 12 décembre 2016 portant création des sociétés d'impact sociétal*, http://data.legilux.public.lu/file/eli_etat-leg-memorial-2016-255-fr-pdf.pdf.

- MTEESS (2021), *Relevé exhaustif des sociétés d'impact sociétal (SIS) agréées par le Ministère du Travail, de l'Emploi et de l'Économie sociale et solidaire (MTEESS)*, https://impotsdirects.public.lu/fr/az/l/libera_dons.html#releveSIS.

- OECD (2019), Better Regulation Practices across the European Union, OECD Publishing, Paris. https://doi.org/10.1787/9789264311732-en.

- ULESS (2017), *Rapport d'activités 2017*, https://www.uless.lu/images/uless/publications/187/docs/MOL_RAPPORT-ULESS-2017-VF-SMALL_PAGE.pdf.

- ULESS (2018), *Rapport d'activités 2018*, https://www.uless.lu/images/uless/publications/218/docs/MOL_RAPPORT-ULESS-2018_VSMALLer.pdf.

- ULESS (2020), *Rapport d'activités 2020*, https://www.uless.lu/images/uless/publications/231/docs/RAPPORT_DACTIVITES_2020.pdf.

www.ingramcontent.com/pod-product-compliance
Lightning Source LLC
Chambersburg PA
CBHW080620270326
41928CB00016B/3145